DISCO DEMOLITION

THE NIGHT DISCO DIED

Steve Dahl with Dave Hoekstra and Paul Natkin

with a Foreword by Bob Odenkirk

CURBSIDE SPLENDOR PUBLISHING

CURBSIDE SPLENDOR PUBLISHING

Published by Curbside Splendor Publishing, Inc., Chicago, Illinois in 2016.

First Edition
Copyright © 2016 by Steve Dahl, Dave Hoekstra, Paul Natkin
Library of Congress Control Number: 2015948128

ISBN 978-1-940430-75-1
Cover photo used with permission by Paul Natkin
Design by Alban Fischer

Manufactured in the United States of America.

www.curbsidesplendor.com

Steve Dahl

4

DISCOGRAPHY

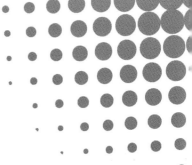

M.C. ANTIL, gofer for Bill Veeck

THAD BOSLEY, 1979 White Sox player who later played for the Cubs, also a soul-gospel musician

ROGER BOSSARD, legendary third-generation groundskeeper at Comiskey Park/U.S. Cellular Field

JOE BRYL, Chicago DJ and cultural historian

MICHAEL CARTOLANO, president of Melrose Pyrotechnics, orchestrated the demolition, has worked with the White Sox since 1959

HARRY WAYNE CASEY, frontman of KC and the Sunshine Band (often credited as the godfathers of disco)

BOB CHICOINE & DAVE GABOREK, Comiskey Park vendors who worked Disco Demolition

JANET DAHL, Steve Dahl's longtime wife and partner

STEVE DAHL, legendary Chicago radio DJ

DENNIS DEYOUNG, co-founder of the popular rock band Styx

TOM DREESEN, comic and fan of Faces, the city's best known disco

DJ LADY D (DARLENE JACKSON), international house music DJ, producer, owner of the D'lectable Music label

ED FARMER, 1979 White Sox player, current team announcer

NANCY FAUST, White Sox organist

TONY FITZPATRICK, Chicago artist, author, and former WLUP radio host

TOM GORSUCH, owner of The Original Mother's, the longest running dance club in America (with Chris Ryan)

KEVIN HICKEY, Chicago restaurateur, fifth-generation Bridgeport resident

JOHN ILTIS, Chicago publicist for WLUP and Disco Demolition

CHAKA KHAN, ten-time Grammy Award winner, R&B and jazz singer from Chicago

KEN KRAVEC, 1979 Chicago White Sox pitcher

TONY LA RUSSA, 1979 White Sox manager

RICHARD LEWIS, comedian

LES GROBSTEIN, reported on the game for the Associated Press, became Steve and Garry's sports reporter

"LORELEI" SHARK, the iconic "rock girl" of The Loop who was at Dahl's side and threw out the first pitch of the double-header

DAVE LOGAN, promotions director at WLUP for Disco Demolition

GARRY MEIER, Chicago rock DJ and co-host of the Steve and Garry Show

MITCH MICHAELS, Chicago rock DJ since 1971

JERRY MICKELSON, co-founder of Jam Productions

PAUL NATKIN, Chicago rock 'n' roll photographer

RICK NIELSEN, guitarist of Cheap Trick

JIM PETERIK, founder of the band Survivor and vocalist for the band Ides of March

JIM RITTENBERG, general manager at Faces

NILE RODGERS, lead guitarist and co-founder of the band Chic and ten-time nominee to the Rock and Roll Hall of Fame

ROMAN J. SAWCZAK, member of Dahl's backup band and producer of the Steve and Garry Show

JACK SCHALLER, owner of Schaller's Pump in Bridgeport

JEFF SCHWARTZ, 1979 WLUP general sales manager and co-creator of Disco Demolition

JOE SHANAHAN, owner of Metro/Smart Bar

ANNE SORKIN, anti-disco crusader and niece of Chicago singer-songwriter John Prine

BOB SIROTT, Chicago radio and television personality

PAUL SULLIVAN, *Chicago Tribune* baseball writer

STEVE TROUT, 1979 White Sox player who later played for the Cubs

MIKE VEECK, organizer and son of late Hall of Famer Bill Veeck

OMAR VIZQUEL, former White Sox shortstop

RICK WOJCIK, South Side native and owner of Dusty Groove record store in Ukrainian Village

Steve Dahl on the field during Disco Demolition

AUTHOR'S NOTE
DAVE HOEKSTRA

Much gratitude to Janet and Steve Dahl for giving the freedom and latitude to share this story. No confines. Plenty of room to dance. And thanks to photographer Paul Natkin for his generosity of spirit.

My father died while I was working on this book. I thought of him a lot. He took me to my first baseball game, 1965, White Sox-Yankees at Comiskey Park. We sat in the right field upper deck and the players seemed so small.

It was a different world . . .

Steve Dahl addresses the crowd at Disco Demolition

 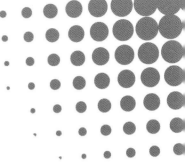

FOREWORD
BOB ODENKIRK

"DISCO DEMOLITION," BY BOB ODENKIRK

Fireworks. clouds of smoke, teenagers.
Beers in hand and the smell of beers a-wafting.
Levi's, mullets, baseball jerseys,
disdain, grievance, and a hint of ultraviolence.
A dream fueled by Italian beef,
steak fries, sliders—
unsettling, with a weird joy coursing through it all.
So sorry they had to cancel game two—oops.

That is my poem about Disco Demolition. I hope you liked it. Nobody asks you to write poetry once you get out of grade school, because it tends to be annoying, but I thought I'd take a hack at it because I am moved by the memory of Disco Demolition Night. Also, I like to make fun of poetry.

MY INTRODUCTION

Disco Demolition was a hoot. It may have been intended as a lark but at some point, a point that no one saw coming, it snowballed into a hoot. From another point of view, it was most certainly a debacle.

Not for me, though. I was and am a big Steve Dahl fan. I lived in Naperville, a quiet and pleasant 'burb. Too quiet and too pleasant, actually. I wanted to rebel against the general ease of it all. Growing up in the Catholic family with the alcoholic dad (yawn), I loved anyone who was saying, "This garbage you see all around you? You got it right, it's all garbage." When you're a teenager, the bullshit detector is fresh out of the box and the batteries are charged full. Steve laughed at pop culture, and his favorite people were my favorite people: John Belushi, Bill Murray, Joe Walsh, funny people with one eyebrow raised at the world. Steve Dahl was anarchy in my UK.

When people ask me why so many funny people come from Chicago, I tell them it's got to do with this chip-on-your-shoulder, eyes-on-the-ground-in-front-of-you, no-smoke-blowing-allowed, rotten attitude. I love it still. (Steve is from California, so I don't know where he came to own his scoffing gaze, and I don't care.) He was the voice inside us, and he did things we wished we could do, like the breakfast club, the parody songs, the prank calls. And he laughed, a lot. Listening to him was fun as hell.

Why did we hate disco? Well, I'd like to start by saying that I also hated Bob Hope and his smarmy double-entendre weirdness, Dean Martin and his phony "I'm a drunk and I don't give a shit" act (believable though, on both counts), and all of that late seventies co-opted hippy culture (the show *That's Incredible!*, the film *Oh God*, the Ford Pinto). It was awful, man. There was a *lot* to hate. But disco music and the culture around it really rose to the occasion. The over-processed sound! The lyrics! The mirrors! The mirror balls! A drug of self-obsession best imbibed off a mirror—what a duo! The seventies needed someone to officially ridicule it, and in Chicago, Steve was the man for the job.

Was it a "homophobic event" at it's core? No. However, there were homophobes in any large group of twelve- to twenty-one-year-old males of that era; quite a few were likely homosexuals who hadn't yet come to joyful acceptance of their true selves. The best argument against this politically-correct twisting of the movement: just listen to Steve's song parody of disco culture "Do Ya Think I'm Disco?" The main character is heterosexual and working hard to let everyone know it. It's a great parody, it tells a story, it's mean-spirited, and it's well-aimed.

Don't trust a teenager who isn't angry. Maybe being angry about the pop culture movement of the moment is an overreaction, but when I watch footage of Disco Demolition, I still feel a connection to that group of teenagers and what happened that night. It was bigger than anything my generation of Chicago kids had seen. And no one expected it. Even if you loved baseball, it was so fun to see something so big and official like a pro baseball game go off the rails. Steve in that army helmet, Jimmy Piersall losing his mind, and those kids—they looked like me and my friends—all those kids walking around in the clouds of lingering smoke, laughing, sliding into base, being stupid and reckless and wild. It still inspires me. I'm glad it happened, and that nobody got too hurt. Vietnam, voting rights, the Democratic [National] Convention [in Grant Park], something truly worthwhile to protest against—was either protested out or not within our limited field of vision. Punk rock had happened, somewhere else, and we were a few years from our Midwest version of it, distinguishable by more self-hatred than anger at the queen of England (I'm talkin' about The Replacements). We worked with what we had.

'Ya proud of yourself, Steve? You should be. This is a great story here: a great night of massive, principled stupidity. I can't wait to read it myself. That's all I can say.

Wait, no, there's one more thing: disco sucks.

Hot
Partly sunny with a
high around 90. Details
on Page 71.

⋄ 1979 by Field Enterprises, Inc.

CHICAGO Sun-Times

Friday, July 13, 1979

15¢ city and suburbs; 25¢ elsewhere

★★★★★
**Turf
Final**

70¢ CTA fare proposed

Gasoline prices going up next week; Page 3

Thousands storm field at Sox park

Thousands of youths taking part in an anti-disco rally swarm on field at Comiskey Park, ignoring the scoreboard sign asking them to "please return to your seats." Police arrived to control crowd that took over the field between games of a White Sox-Detroit Tigers doubleheader. They set bonfires and damaged turf, causing second-game postponement. Stories on Page 8 and Back Page. (Sun-Times Photo by Don Bierman)

The front page of the *Chicago Sun-Times* on July 13, 1979, the day after Disco Demolition. Courtesy of Sun-Times Media.

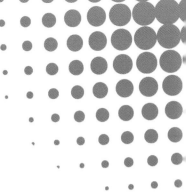

INTRODUCTION

STEVE DAHL

Steve Dahl was twenty-four years old on July 12, 1979, the night of Disco Demolition.
This is his preface in his own words:

I t was a very different time for Chicago than it was for London or New York City. This sturdy midwestern town was not hosting late night clubs with red ropes. It was only rock 'n' roll, and that's the way the young kids liked it. They had their T-shirts and their ripped jeans, their long hair and their longneck beers. Their music heroes played rough and loud. These kids did not wish to be tamed or curated. Their parents had Paul Anka and Andy Williams; Mom and Dad had shaken their heads at Elvis and his gyrations. Loud anthemic music was functioning as a rite of passage: a sure way to push back from adults. Every generation has its rebellion, and rock 'n' roll was providing a soundtrack for the seventies.

Then Tony Manero was created. He was born from an article by a British writer who identified the disco world as the "new Saturday night in New York." [*Saturday Night Fever*] was a smash, the soundtrack exploded. The principle of crossing from being a nobody to a somebody, as pictured in the film, seemed to demand a repudiation of all things rough—like rock 'n' roll and bar nights. Chicago kids liked their Saturday nights just as they had been experiencing them. Dress up? No. Dance lessons? No. Cover charge? Hell no. The Bee Gees had popped out a bouncy album, and the girls were ready to dress up, twirl, and be twirled. The storyline seemed to demean the ordinary life that kids inhabited in favor of Manhattan glitz. No.

If anything, the pushback from disco saturation was an act of self-preservation. No kid, just figuring out who he was and where he was going, would be prepared to have his assimilated rock 'n' roll identity stripped from him. If the resistance was furious, it was because they were not prepared to shuck the uniform that sheltered them in their transition from kid to adult.

I'm worn out from defending myself as a racist homophobe for fronting Disco Demolition at Comiskey Park. This event was not racist, not anti-gay. It is important to me that this is viewed from the lens of 1979. That evening was a declaration of independence from the tyranny of sophistication. I like to think of it as illustrative of the power that radio has to create community and share similarities and frustrations. It is for that magic that I wish to keep the memory severed from those who ascribe hateful motives to a wildly successful radio promotion.

We were just kids pissing on a musical genre. We were choosing to remain faithful to the bands that provided the backdrop to our lives.

And so, when Rod Stewart strutted to "Do Ya think I'm Sexy" and Mick Jagger preened to "Miss You," it seemed the rock loyalty might be one-sided. Their heroes were appropriating disco beats and fancy dress codes. A further rebuke to the Chicago rock 'n' roll lifestyle happened in January 1979, when legacy rock radio station WDAI fired me to become a disco-only station. I had only been in Chicago for twelve months, but Chicago kids had grown up with WDAI, from the British Invasion onward. They felt stripped of something essential to their formative years. Their rage and resistance was directed at no ethnic group or sexual orientation; the loss of the station was simply a repudiation of their still-evolving psyches.

I got a job at The Loop, a rock 'n' roll altar. Callers welcomed me with warm wishes and the mantra, "disco sucks." They were passionate about their music and their lifestyles. I tapped into it, both as a response to being canned to make room for disco, and to build a community so I could keep my job. My take was always based in humor, pointing out the discomfort of having to dress a part to go to a bar.

I borrowed Rod Stewart's music and recreated "Do Ya Think I'm Sexy" as my anthem. The visuals were highly entertaining, but had no connection to sexual orientation or color.

> *I wear tight pants*
> *I always stuff a sock in*
> *It always makes*
> *the ladies start to talking*
> *My shirt is open*
> *I never use the buttons*
> *Though I look hip, I work for EF Hutton . . .*

Do you think I'm disco
'Cuz I spend so much time
Blowing out my hair?
Do you think I'm disco,
'Cuz I know the dance steps
Learned them all at Fred Astaire?

Not a masterpiece, I know, and not a piece of social commentary. Just a few laughs at the guys a few years older who were willing to costume up to get in with the trendy elite. Some of them were older brothers, or the guy who danced away with your girl.

We were letting off a little steam. We were relaxing in our corduroy jeans and T-shirts. We were not quite ready to dress for success or give up our clattering soundtrack for disco beats. I never wanted to mount or lead a social movement. I wanted to entertain and to provide a release for kids who had too little money and too much awkwardness for the dance world. I wanted to say, *The music you revere is great, and you are okay just as you are.*

It is the right of each generation to declare, "This is who I am." And to dance to the beat they choose to dance to—even if it *is* only head thrashing.

What follows is an oral history of the events preceding and following Disco Demolition, a look at Chicago culture circa 1979, and how Chicago house music followed disco. This book was written in the context of that period. And everything is on the record.

Steve Dahl salutes his Anti Disco Army

PREFACE
DAVE HOEKSTRA

O n July 12, 1979, the Chicago rock 'n' roll station WLUP-FM and the Chicago White Sox collaborated on a twi-night double-header originally called "Teen Night."

After the events of the evening, it became known as "Disco Demolition." Fans who brought a disco record to Comiskey Park would be admitted for ninety-eight cents (FM 97.9 was WLUP's "The Loop" position on the dial) to see the Detroit Tigers play the White Sox.

In the center of the country, American music was at a crossroads.

And Comiskey Park was a rock 'n' roll Gettysburg. What followed was one of the greatest promotions in the history of Major League Baseball. The White Sox had been averaging about 20,000 fans a night in a grand old stadium that seated close to 50,000. Neither team was very sexy in the standings. The White Sox were 40-46, in fifth place in the American League's Western Division. The Tigers were 41-44 in fifth place in the Eastern Division.

About 70,000 people showed up for the game.

Security quickly got out of hand as the audience discovered vinyl records made great Frisbees. Several players rightly remarked they were afraid of getting hurt by a Commodores single. After the White Sox lost the first game 4-1, the promotion took place in center field. WLUP morning personality General Steve Dahl and his sidekick Garry Meier led their Insane Coho Lips Army to center field to blow up a large box of disco records. They were assisted by WLUP's provocative "Goddess of Fire" Lorelei Shark as General Dahl led the crowd in chants of "disco sucks!"

When the records blew up, the audience flooded the field. Fans tore out seats. Bonfires were lit with pocket lighters. Chicago police arrived at White Sox Park on horseback. The second game was canceled. Disco Demolition became the first and only event other than an act of God to cause the cancellation of a Major League Baseball game. (The Cleveland Indians' "Ten Cent Beer Night" in June of 1974 also resulted in a riot; the game was forfeited in the ninth inning.)

White Sox president Bill Veeck was the king of baseball promotions. In 1976, the White Sox were ready to move to Seattle, until Veeck bought the team from John Allyn. One of Veeck's promotions during his inaugural year was outfitting his players in clam diggers and hot pants. No trend was too small for Veeck. And in 1979, there was Disco Demolition. "I was amazed," Veeck said afterwards. "We had anticipated 32,000 to 35,000. We had more security than we ever had before. But we had as many people in here as we ever had." The security at Disco Demolition was as innocent as a Dan Fogelberg song compared to that of U.S. Cellular Field in the summer of 2015.

The passage of time has shed a different light on Disco Demolition; the events can be refitted to today's values. Dahl told me, "Most of the people calling it racist and homophobic are younger and have come out of college predisposed to think that thanks to identity politics."

The front page headline of the July 13, 1979 *Chicago Tribune* sports section read, "When fans wanted to rock, the baseball stopped," and columnist David Israel wrote, "Ten years after Woodstock, there was Veeckstock . . . As far as riots go, this one was fairly lovely. I mean, it isn't going to make anyone forget Grant Park or the Days of Rage. It was a lot of sliding into second base and 'Look-at-me-Ma' jumping around for the benefit of the television camera." After all, the Sister Sledge disco tune "We Are Family," co-written by Nile Rodgers, was one of the hits of the summer of 1979. (It even became the theme song for the Pittsburgh Pirates.)

On the flip side, in December 1979, rock critic Dave Marsh wrote of Disco Demolition in *Rolling Stone*, "White males eighteen to thirty-four are the most likely to see disco as the product of homosexuals, blacks, and Latins and therefore they're the most likely to respond to appeals to wipe out such threats to their security."

Veeck was a pioneer in the civil rights movement. He joined the NAACP (National Association for the Advancement of Colored People) not long after he purchased the Cleveland Indians in 1946. He hired African Americans to work in all parts of Cleveland Municipal Stadium, from beer vendors up through the front office. In 1947, he made Larry Doby the first African American baseball player in the American League, and in 1948, Veeck signed Negro League-legend Satchel Paige. New York's *New Amsterdam News* called Veeck "The Abe Lincoln of Baseball."

Disco Demolition was about class structure and music. At one time, disco was full of adventure and risk, like its offspring house music. Disco's roots are full of integrity, ranging from the breathy raps of Isaac Hayes to the lean uptempo arrangements of Kenneth Gamble and Leon Huff. The 1974 Gamble-Huff MFSB instrumental "TSOP (The Sound of Philadelphia)" is regarded as one of the primal disco hits. But by 1979, much of disco was defined by excess.

That summer, disco was dancing in an air of testosterone. John Wayne, America's cowboy, died that June, and Ronald Reagan was in the bullpen for the 1980 election. Burt Reynolds had been named the best box office attraction in the country (1977 through 1981) in a poll of movie exhibitors.

During the summer of 1979, I was writing for a suburban Chicago newspaper while exploring the periphery of urban music. I loved the reggae-punk sound of The Clash and discovered the electric funkateer who called himself Prince. I was a huge Faces fan and was repulsed with the Rod Stewart hit "Do Ya' Think I'm Sexy?"

That's what led me to Disco Demolition.

I liked the Latin-tinged "disco" music of Tavares, the soul of the Ohio Players and the best orgasmic stuff from Donna Summer. But rock 'n' rollers crossing over into disco was wrong. Much later I would find out "Do Ya' Think I'm Sexy" lifted the melody from the composition "Taj Mahal" by Brazilian artist Jorge Ben Jor. Jor filed a copyright infringement lawsuit against Stewart and the case was settled amicably.

I love baseball more than Faces and the Stones, so it was easy to fork over ninety-eight cents on July 12, 1979, to catch the White Sox play a double-header with the Detroit Tigers. I liked Steve Dahl and Garry Meier. Their candor and real life approach is what made them appealing to an army of seekers and dissenters.

In 1979 I was living in an apartment a block east of Wrigley Field and dating a woman called Miller. She was from the far South Side neighborhood of Beverly and had eight sisters and one brother, a full starting line up of Sox fans. I was a Cubs fan. Miller and I took the El down from the North Side and got to the park early. I don't recall seeing the thousands of people who later gathered on the outskirts of Old Comiskey Park. It was a hot, steamy night. We sat in the upper deck in right field. I behaved myself, likely because I didn't drink Schlitz or Stroh's, the Comiskey house beers.

The dimly lit upper cavern at Comiskey invited anarchy even on the quietest of nights. It was a good place to make out, guzzle from open bottles of Jack Daniel's, and ignore the game. My father, who worked in the nearby Union Stockyards as a young man, took me to my first Major League Baseball game at Comiskey: White Sox-Yankees, 1965, with Mickey Mantle stumbling around on his last, weary legs.

The White Sox had a 40-46 record on July 12, 1979, and were not a very notable team. Disco Demolition may never have happened had the White Sox been compelling to watch.

Left fielder Ralph "Roadrunner" Garr had seen his best days with the Atlanta Braves and no longer deserved the nickname. Right fielder Claudell Washington became a punch line of a bad joke. (But he hit three home runs in a game on July 14, perhaps inspired by Disco Demolition). With such a blank canvas, WMAQ-AM radio announcers Harry Caray and former major leaguer Jimmy Piersall became the life of the party.

Owner Veeck would do anything to bring fans into the park to see his mundane cast of characters. Only a month before Disco Demolition, Veeck presented "Disco Night," holding a dance contest before a game against the Seattle Mariners (according to a 1979 White Sox program I saved). June 23 was Lithuanian Day and August 20 was "Beer Case Stacking" Day. Veeck knew his South Side audience.

Former White Sox pitcher Ken Kravec said, "We had a good year in 1977, and Veeck was promoting. I was warming up in the bullpen when it was 'Belly Dancer Night.' There were thousands of belly dancers. They opened up the center field gates and here they come. As they come through the gate, some belly dancers go left and some go right. You had to track around the field. I'm warming up, no big deal. All of a sudden they walk between me and the catcher. I asked security, 'Can you get them to walk over by the side so I can keep warming up?' Something was happening almost every night."

The White Sox lost the first game of the Disco Demolition double-header 4-1 on a nifty five-hitter from the Tigers' Pat Underwood, a native of Kokomo (not the Beach Boys city) Indiana. Between games, Dahl entered the field on a Commando Jeep as the leader of the "Insane Coho Lips," his anti-disco army, joined by Lorelei. Dahl wore military fatigues and a crooked helmet.

Dahl and Lorelei landed at second base and led the crowd in chants of "disco sucks!" There was a box of disco records on the outfield side of second base. Many fans took records to their seats. Then the records were blown up, and all hell broke loose.

About fifteen minutes before the second game was to begin, fans stormed the field. I didn't throw my Rod Stewart record on the field; I had given it to the ticket taker. My clearest memory of that night is the cloud of smoke that hung over the field. "Beer and baseball go together; they have for years," said the late Tigers manager Sparky Anderson. "But I think those kids were doing other things than [drinking] beer."

Once the riot began, Miller and I departed immediately. There was no pushing or shoving to get out of "The Baseball Palace of the World." Maybe most of the fans were on the field.

Thirty-nine fans were arrested on charges of disorderly conduct, but there were no reported injuries. At first, the second game was postponed, but American League President Lee MacPhail ordered a forfeit to the Tigers the following day. It would be the last forfeit in Major League Baseball until 1995, when Los Angeles Dodgers' fans threw souvenir baseballs on the field, resulting in a forfeit to the St. Louis Cardinals. The announced attendance for the Disco Demolition game was 47,795 people. Bill Veeck guessed that between 50,000 and 55,000 people were in the ballpark. The capacity of Comiskey Park was 44,492. Chicago police were worried that crowds outside would also riot, but that never happened. Over time, Disco Demolition assumed the fable-like characteristics that are so common to baseball: 70,000 people were in the ballpark; 10,000 people were on the Dan Ryan Expressway in front of the ballpark. It was big, but not that big.

After the game, Sox pitcher Richard Wortham told reporters he was a fan of Waylon Jennings and Willie Nelson, and then added, "This wouldn't have happened if they had country and western night."

Wortham's teammate Thaddis Bosley, Jr. is one of the most thoughtful of the more than fifty people I interviewed for this book. Born in Southern California in 1956, his fourteen-year Major League Baseball career included stops with the Chicago Cubs (1983–86) and the White Sox (1978–80). After Bosley retired in 1990 he became a coach for the Oakland Athletics and hitting coach for the Texas Rangers. Bosley continues to pursue his first love of songwriting, releasing original songs in vintage soul and gospel genres. He writes poetry in his spare time.

Bosley split the 1979 season between the White Sox and their Class AAA affiliate in Iowa. He hit .312 in thirty-six games for the White Sox while battling injuries.

"I remember Disco Demolition, but truthfully I don't remember if I was physically there," he told me in September 2015 on a break from his job as executive director of athletics at Grace University, a private Christian school in Omaha, Nebraska. Such honesty is a good sign. Today, everyone says they were there. "Some of the guys told me how afraid they were," he continued. "I specifically recall that during that time there was a tremendous transition of musicology. From an industry standpoint there seemed to be a push into disco music even though traditional rockers weren't into that. The backdrop of the Comiskey event had some of those undertones. People said it was racially motivated. I don't know if it was or not, but there certainly was a divide into what traditional rock should be versus disco."

Bosley was traded from the California Angels to the White Sox in 1977. He played for the White Sox from 1978 until the spring of 1981 when he was traded to Milwaukee. In 1983, he was traded back to Chicago, this time to play for the Cubs.

"Chicago was a whole new dynamic for me," Bosley said. "I had never experienced segregation like that. Chicago in the late seventies was very stressful for me. Then the whole Comiskey Park incident, you know how things implode? It seemed like things exploded in terms of what was really going on, not only in the cities but in the nation as a whole, as far as music was concerned.

"The thing that fascinated me the most about the event is that, boom, the next day disco died."

Bosley got quiet as he collected his thoughts. "After that there was a shift. When I was traded to the Cubs I ended up buying a place in downtown Chicago and lived there for twenty-three years. That's a reflection of how much the shift occurred. Harold Washington became mayor of the city (in 1983). A lot of good things birthed themselves out of that experience, out of that time."

Steve Dahl with a box of disco records waiting to be blown up

Fans wait to enter Comiskey Park the day of Disco Demolition

I. MIKE AND BILL VEECK

Every good story has a point of conflict. Steve Dahl's career ascended after Disco Demolition. Mike Veeck's career crashed, and never really recovered.

Bill Veeck, Jr. took the blame for Disco Demolition.

The elder Veeck sold the White Sox two years after the event and spent the last summers of his life in the center field bleachers at Wrigley Field. Veeck died of cancer in 1986 at the age of seventy-one and was inducted into the Baseball Hall of Fame in 1991.

"The first time I came into Comiskey was the last time I felt safe in this world," his son, Mike Veeck, said during a conversation on a rainy spring afternoon at U.S. Cellular Field in 2015. "I remember holding Dad's hand and seeing this beautiful green diamond in the midst of all this macadam. It seemed like he knew everybody in the world. Everybody said, 'Hi Bill!' It was the most wonderful thing."

Mike Veeck had a promising career in Major League Baseball until the night of the promotion.

"I'm the one who triggered it," Veeck said. "My old man did what a good leader does. He took the heat. For ten years it was very painful for me. Steve Dahl's career took off. I couldn't get a job in baseball. I was red hot with soccer clubs because they like riots, and every radio station in the world wanted me as a promo director. I went to hang drywall in Florida. I got divorced. I never wanted to hear the phone ring again.

"Why do you think I disappeared at the bottom of a bottle for ten years? I drank two bottles of VO a day, Extra Calvert was my favorite, not the Lord Calvert. My Dad was the only person in the ballpark who understood exactly how I felt. We weren't the greatest father and son, in terms of Ward Cleaver. But professional to professional there was nobody better, and he knew this was one that got away—from everybody. I know the event stung my Dad."

Actually, Veeck didn't even have the soccer crowd.

In the aftermath of the event, the late Chicago Sting soccer team owner Lee Stern said in the *Chicago Tribune*, "When I heard about the success of this Dahl guy and his anti-disco nights, we looked at the possibility of having him come to one of our games. But after seeing that weirdo on TV tonight, there's no way we'd do it now."

Veeck sat in the open air patio at U.S. Cellular Field as we talked. Members of the Cincinnati Reds were running laps. Yes, the Reds who beat the White Sox in the 1919 World Series, rigged by gamblers. The series is on record. It was worse than Disco Demolition.

"I never talk like this, you know this," Veeck said. "I invented skyboxes. I was on fire in 1979. I was twenty-eight and every day was an idea. I never thought I would be judged on one promotion. These private party areas that are the background of sports marketing? They were invented here." Bill Veeck, Jr.'s "Picnic Area" was created at Old Comiskey Park, across the street from the site of Disco Demolition. It became known as "The World's Largest Saloon."

"Every area of Old Comiskey that wasn't being utilized, we turned into a money maker," Veeck said. "It changed the way sports was marketed. Comiskey had the old Chicago Cardinals press box." The forlorn Cardinals press box was along the third base line attached to the roof of the ball park.

Veeck nodded at the sky over the empty ball park and continued. "I looked up there one night when I was shooting fireworks and there was the press box in the reflection. You would go to the press box and get two cases of Stroh's and a rib dinner. Dad was trying to sign (outfielder) Chester Lemon. He needed 70,000 dollars. I said, 'We're going to sell that Cardinals press box.' He said, 'What are we going to call it?' They had 'Owners Boxes' in the great Astrodome. When I saw the reflections in the fireworks I said, 'Let's call it a skybox.' There wasn't even a bathroom in it, which is why you only got two cases of beer. My dad got 70,000 dollars in seventy-two hours. It was a great thing. He said, 'It's a terrible idea, Mike.' I said, 'Why is that? I created money out of nothing.' He said, 'It's elitist.' I didn't see that.

I was doing something for my dad."

Veeck sighed. Sometimes it's difficult for Veeck to talk about his father. "People acted like Disco Demolition was the first besmirching of my dad's career," he continued. "Well, they don't know much about the Veeck history, going back to Capone days. He testified for a character in Cleveland who buried the 1949 pennant in Cleveland and got murdered the next day."

Later in life, Bill Veeck became the only Major League Baseball owner to testify on behalf of Curt Flood in the outfielder's 1970 lawsuit against the organization.

His son said, "When you're a legend, all of that goes away."

Mike Veeck

M.C. Antil worked in the White Sox group sales department in the late 1970s. "The media was taking dead aim on the event," Antil reflected. "Bill deflected all the blame and said, 'This was mine.' That stuck with me—his willingness to stand in front of media to shield Mike from it. It's something that isn't talked about. Bill didn't have anything to do with Disco Demolition, he was trying to run a baseball team and Mike was running the business side of it."

"That was real noble of Bill," said WLUP-FM's 1979 Promotion Director Dave Logan. "It is important that Mike Veeck is noted as someone who had the balls to do this. He got hosed."

Mike Veeck did not listen to WLUP. He liked the wide range of pop, rock, and R&B on AM radio, a child of WLS and WCFL radio. "Somebody told me there was a guy blowing up disco records on the air," Veeck recalled. "So I couldn't get to the station fast enough. I'm scaling the Hancock building. I went to call on Dahl when he got off the air. I didn't have any idea it was going to draw. Dahl didn't know if it was going to draw. Four thousand people would be fine as far as I was concerned. We did Disco Night in 1977 and drew 20,000 people, and there were about twenty dance clubs from around town. That was the night the seeds of anti-disco or whatever you want to call it were sewn."

After the Disco Night game, Veeck ushered a group of White Sox front office staff to Miller's Pub, a favorite Loop watering hole of Bill Veeck. Schemes and dreams about music, baseball, and promotions lasted until 3:00 a.m.

"We said, 'Let's do a night for people who love rock 'n' roll and never thought about it again,'" Veeck recalled. "Jeff Schwartz (WLUP's General Sales Manager in 1979) and I were the ones who never let it die. I didn't have a relationship with Dahl but I worked a lot with Schwartz; he had a lot of product and a lot of records. Then Schwartz went to work for Heftel (WLUP). A little known fact is that Heftel hired me a few weeks before the event to do the sports on Dahl's show.

"I lost that gig, too."

Longtime Chicago sportscaster Les Grobstein replaced Mike Veeck. In May, 1979 WLS News Director Reed Pence asked Grobstein for an audition tape. "Reed said I had the inside track," Grobstein said. "I called back in June and he said they were getting close. Eventually he called back and said, 'We have our sportscaster.' I thought it was me. He said, 'Are you sitting down?'"

It was Mike Veeck.

Grobstein was incredulous. "I said, Mike Veeck knows as much about doing a sportscast as I know about owning a baseball team. Mike did a handful of shows. He never mentioned the Cubs or Bears training camp. All he did was a commercial for the White Sox. Then Disco Demolition happened and he disappeared." Grobstein finally debuted on Larry Lujack and Bob Sirott's shows in October 1979 and remained at WLS-AM until December 1989.

Jeff Schwartz had been at WLUP for a year by the time Disco Demolition rolled around. Schwartz is a native of the Albany Park neighborhood of Chicago, where he went to elementary school with Bob Sirott. During the mid-1980s, Schwartz was an advertising consultant of the now defunct Flipside Records and was the cartoon character "Mr. Cheap" in the chain's advertising campaign.

"We had the hottest station in town," Schwartz said in a summer 2015 interview in Los Angeles. At the time, he was Vice President of Strategic Corporate Marketing for Yahoo! Sports Radio. "I get a call from Mike Veeck. The team was struggling. We met at Yes Sir, Senator (the now defunct Barney's Market Place restaurant in the West Loop). I was a big fan of reefer and a couple of other light substances. So I'm smoking a reefer on the way to the restaurant and Mike Veeck was there with (Bill Veeck's assistant and idea man) Rudie Schaffer's son David, who was head of security. They're drinking. I never drank but I was pretty stoned. They said, 'We gotta do a promotion together.' I really liked Mike and Schaffer's kid. We were having a nice steak dinner. True, and no disrespect to anybody, the exact words I said [were], 'You have the exploding scoreboard, right? And I've got Dahl in the morning blowing up disco records. Is there any way we could take that to the field as a promotion?' And I left the rest of the thinking up to them. Dahl and I did not have the greatest relationship.

"Dahl and I had as good a relationship as you could with Steve."

Sirott said, "I was well aware of Jeff's involvement with Disco Demolition. I think Jeff was stoned in the third grade. I remember he had one of the first head shops with the blue light in the neighborhood. He's always been someone who was into analyzing show business. When we were in grade school, maybe it was after Jack Parr left *The Tonight Show* and before Johnny Carson became host, they had guest hosts take over *The Tonight Show*. At recess Jeff would be holding court analyzing the pros and cons of how this person did as host of *The Tonight Show*. He was into show business."

But it was Mike Veeck who took the heat, as he continued to reminisce at U.S. Cellular Field.

"It was all my fault," Veeck said. "I knew there was going to be 35,000 people. That was the number I gave the police. The morning of the game I said to security, 'We're going to have 35,000.' They thought that was the funniest thing, when the club is averaging 21,000." (According to Major League Baseball, the average was 20,458.)

"The mistake came with Old Comiskey: portable ticket booths out front. Guys who are in their [mid-sixties] now are in portable ticket booths. The security guys call me and say the kids outside trying to get in [the park] are rattling the portable ticket booths. The old guys are worried and anxious. So we moved fifteen [security guards] from the field out there. Crowd control is a misnomer. You rely on the idea that the crowd never thinks as one. Our crowd was already stirred up. The place was packed. They see fifteen yellow jackets leave the field and this was one time they thought as one: 'That idiot Veeck moved security out, let's go on the field.' It was perfectly logical. It was my mistake.

"The next day the commissioner's office, the Bowie of Kuhn sends out a memo about 'no negative promotions' because it was anti-disco."

It took Veeck a decade to move in a positive direction.

In November 1989, he joined The Goldklang Group (including Marv Goldklang and actor Bill Murray) and in 1990 became team president of the Miami Miracle, helping relocate the team to Fort Myers, Florida, in 1992. Today the Goldkang Group owns and operates the minor league Charleston RiverDogs (Veeck is president, although he does not have ownership), the St. Paul Saints, and the collegiate baseball team Pittsfield Suns. Veeck also has an interest in the Normal, Illinois CornBelters and the River City Rascals, outside of St. Louis and separate from the Goldklang group.

In 2005, Veeck wrote a book, *Fun is Good: How to Create Joy and Passion in Your Workplace & Career*. Wilmette, Illinois born Bill Murray contributed the blurb, "Fun should be the driving force behind most any decision."

Veeck arrived in Charleston in 1997, and staged "Bill Murray Night," "Drag Queen Night," and "Nobody Night," which insisted no fans were allowed to enter the padlocked ballpark, at Joseph P. Riley, Jr. Park. And now his son, Mike "Night Train" Veeck, named after the late Detroit Lions linebacker Dick "Night Train" Lane, is a White Sox executive in charge of fan engagement.

Veeck used to receive roughly twenty-five requests a year to stage Disco Demolition II. He consistently declined, but on July 19, 2014, after a RiverDogs game at Joseph P. Riley, Jr. Park, he blew up Justin Bieber and Miley Cyrus records on the field. Grainy footage of the original Disco Demolition was shown on the center field scoreboard. In a heartfelt speech after the game, Veeck thanked the sold out crowd of more than 6,000 fans for giving him a new start in life.

During the summer of 2015, Veeck reflected, "Disco Demolition made me great at what I did the rest of my life. Until then I really believed that you can control something. That taught me the greatest lesson. It made me relax and made me take chances. Control anything? I don't think so.

"In the late 1980s they had a twenty-five-year retrospective on rock 'n' roll. They used Disco Demolition to end the first half of this look back. I'm laying on a couch at a place I'm renting. I had my son Wednesday night and Saturday. Never missed a day. I had a sodie pop with my landlord. She was rough. Finally I looked around and said, 'Disco Demolition was a cultural event.'"

One sunny day in early May 2015, Omar Vizquel, coach of the Detroit Tigers and former White Sox shortstop, hailed a cab with his wife from their downtown hotel and headed to the Northwest Side to visit Paul Natkin. Vizquel wanted to see Natkin's photographs of Disco Demolition.

Vizquel played in the major leagues for twenty-four years but had seen nothing like this. "I'm interested in this from a historical point of view," Vizquel said, flipping through more than fifty black and white Disco Demolition photographs. "I've never heard of anything like this at a baseball game. I never heard of such a commotion where you bring your LP, throw it in a box and blow it up. Obviously the whole thing went crazy.

Omar Vizquel

"I was twelve years old in 1979. I lived in Venezuela, but I didn't know about [Disco Demolition] until [2014] when I saw the ESPN special. I saw Paul [in the Commando Jeep], holding on and snapping pictures. I thought, 'How cool would it be if I can get ahold of this guy and he can show me some of the stuff he shot that day? He was right in the middle of the action. So I called (White Sox photographer) Ron [Vesley] to help me find Paul."

Vizquel played more games as shortstop than anyone in baseball history. He is an eclectic athlete in the manner of Cubs manager Joe Maddon and NBA Hall of Famers Phil Jackson and Kareem Abdul-Jabbar. Vizquel is not defined by a singular style. "I've always been curious," he explained. "I ask my players to go to museums and galleries with me. They're not interested. In August, they are doing a *Dancing With Stars* salsa contest for charity in Detroit. They are looking for players to participate in the event—all they have to do is dance with beautiful girls for two minutes. How many players do you think wrote their name down? One. So I had to write my name down.

"Salsa is more in my blood than disco. When I first heard disco in Venezuela I was eight years old. We saw the movies like *Thank God It's Friday* with Donna Summer and even *Grease* with John Travolta. You could dance to the music. I like so many different things, baseball sometimes looks secondary. You like pictures, music, architectural work. Why do you have to buy a piece of furniture for 1,500 dollars when you can put it together yourself for 300 dollars? The process of getting there is even more exciting."

Vizquel collects photographs and vintage cameras and plays drums. He draws and paints portraits with water colors, including a portrait of Tigers coach and former White Sox manager Gene Lamont.

A Seattle resident, Vizquel does not hear much disco in the Tigers' clubhouse. "There's lots of EDM (Electronic Dance Music)," said Vizquel, whose walk-up music included Led Zeppelin's "Black Dog" and "The Immigrant Song" to honor his Venezuelan roots. "We play 'Fireball' by Pit Bull when we win. Every team I know has a song they play after they win. Last year was (DJ Snake's) 'Turn Down For What.' As far as disco coming back, that's weird. I listen to all kinds of music, but mostly rock 'n' roll. When I was a kid I loved KISS. They play a little bit of 'Detroit Rock City' in Detroit and that's kind of cool.

"But to see what happened on that day of Disco Demolition? People were ripping shirts off each other. Short shorts on the field. Guys burning stuff in the outfield. They stole home plate. I've seen fights and burning stuff in the stands in Venezuela, but never anything like this on that night in Chicago."

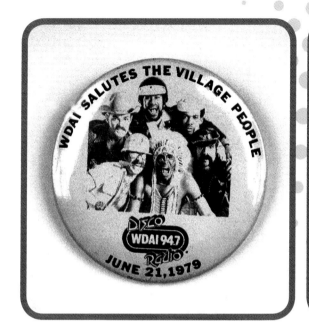

Anti-Disco Army and WDAI promotional buttons

Steve and Janet Dahl 1979 Christmas Card photo

2. JANET AND STEVE DAHL
A TEAM FOR THE AGES

On August 11, 1978, less than a year before Disco Demolition, Janet Joliat married Steve Dahl. They have endured the magnitude of Disco Demolition, Steve's battle with alcoholism, job instability. The Dahls have raised three wonderful sons.

None of the Dahls like disco.

Janet Dahl sat alone on the sofa in their southwest suburban Chicago home. "[Steve is] introverted. I don't think a lot of people know him really well. He's not comfortable in the world." She looked around the living room and continued, "This is his safe house. He is very happy with a snack tray and a television set. Steve married everything he wasn't; he was uneducated and he married a teacher going to law school. He was shy and he married a blabber. He had a very dysfunctional family and he married into this grounded Irish-German family. I was a lifeline for him and he was an adventure for me.

"The disco thing was very validating for him. He was speaking. And someone was listening. It wasn't about causing trouble and making money. He was uncomfortable doing it. He looked goofy and chubby, his hair was bad, and he was breaking records on his head. But to be embraced was validating for someone like him.

"He was honored he was touching people. And he was touched back."

Janet Joliat grew up in Royal Oak, Michigan. Her father Tom sold heating and air conditioning systems for commercial buildings, while her mother Elaine raised Janet and her five siblings. In 1976, Janet was twenty-six years old, teaching at Bloomfield Hills Junior High School. She listened to Steve Dahl on WABX-FM during her morning commute.

"Detroit was a hard rocking town," she said. "I felt an affiliation with his music selections. He played California rock. The first time I heard Bruce Springsteen, he was playing it. I was dating his best friend, and we met that way. And the next thing you know, I was dating him."

Janet and Steve owned similar record collections. They had albums by the Eagles. Jackson Browne. Dan Fogelberg. She said, "We were compatible, but he had been in a very short marriage and sort of ran away from home. He needed nurturing. My parents weren't happy. He was bouncing from station to station.

"When we started dating he seemed vulnerable. All of his bravado seemed fake to me. He'd come to Detroit in a hideous turquoise Subaru with an after market air conditioner. When I'd see him rolling around in that car, I'd think, 'That is the stupidest car I've ever seen.' I wanted my radio guy to be more glamorous than this car. So he saved all his money and bought a 1976 BMW. It was Band-Aid brown, it looked dumb, and he paid a lot of money for it. But it was, 'I'm a DJ now; I'm hip and I have this car.'

Steve and Janet dated for eighteen months before getting married.

It hasn't been easy, but they stayed together for their children. Patrick, thirty-five, works Banner Collective, a branch of the Wirtz Corporation; Michael, thirty-three, is a producer at the Leo Burnett advertising agency; Matthew, thirty-one, is a video editor at Mr. Skin and a firefighter in LaGrange Park.

"Steve comes from an alcoholic mom and dad and an alcoholic brother," she said. "He didn't know anything else. He had no idea about a family life. I didn't even realize he was an alcoholic. I was probably the classic enabler because I didn't see the signs. I was left to raise the kids. He slept in the morning. Worked in the afternoon. Drank after work. Sobered up and came home. It was hard. He went from being a compensating drinker where he would get jolly and hang out with people to becoming really vitriolic. It was like his liver decided not to filter anymore. He knew he was on borrowed time. He had to stop. We had a thirteen-year-old who was taking notes. It was getting harder to say, 'Dad's got the flu.' But Steve is shy, and for ten years it was a good social lubricant for him. And then for five years it was a terrible deterioration where he was angry and kind of lost. It was very dark. Those were the years surrounding the end of the Steve and Garry [Meier] partnership.

"But I was not ready to give up."

And then Dahl quit drinking.

It was June 24, 1995, during rehearsal for the next evening's Navy Pier concert with Steve Dahl & the Dahlfins with special guest Brian Wilson of the Beach Boys. "I just stopped," Dahl said in a separate interview. "I didn't think I would be able to help my boys make it through high school with 'Do as I say, not as I do.'"

Janet's resolve was wavering. The Dahl boys were entering their rebellious teenage years. "I'm a sleeper and he's an insonmniac," she said. "After he stopped [drinking], for eight years he was up every night until they were home. He knew what to look for. They would have gamed me so much, but Steve was right there."

Former White Sox left hander Ken Kravec was scheduled to start the second game of the Disco Demolition double-header. "I used to listen to Steve Dahl every morning," Kravec said in an interview. "Every day he talked about how he hated disco. He was way ahead of his time as a 'Shock Jock.' I did the White Sox fantasy camps for over twenty years. [In 2010], they brought in Steve Dahl for the fantasy camp."

Dahl played first base, coached by the late pitcher Kevin Hickey and former outfielder Harold Baines. "You thought some crazy guy was going to show up with a shtick still playing that role," Kravec said. "But he was older, more mature and mellow. He obviously had moved on and went down a different road. Good for him."

Roman J. Sawczak was guitarist and musical director for Dahl's band Teenage Radiation in the 1980s. He played on the "Do Ya' Think I'm Disco" recording, and during the mid-1980s, he was executive producer for Dahl and Meier's radio show on WLUP. Sawczak knew Dahl very well, but now they rarely speak.

"The day I heard he sobered up, I was so happy," Sawczak said from his home in Dyer, Indiana. "I guarantee you he would not be here today. Steve was an extremist. When he was good, I don't know if I've known anybody more generous. But I don't know if I worked with anybody that's been more of a jerk. Now I imagine it's not as much up and down. We were doing cool gigs with Teenage Radiation, and we'd do two hours. One time at the Park West I think we played three songs. He'd start drinking and going off on tangents. Then when we got to the song, we'd have to stop and start because he forgot the words. We'd stand there and go, 'Is this any fun anymore?' And it wasn't. But I have no hard feelings on Steve about anything. I'm more grateful and thankful than ever.

"And disco still sucks."

Darlene Jackson, known internationally as DJ Lady D, is considered a house music pioneer. She also happens to be a producer, owner of the D'lectable Music label, and a single mother. She has played Lollapalloza in Chicago and performed disco and techno sets in Asia and Europe.

In the mid-1990s, Jackson was working as a suite attendant for a Ringling Brothers Barnum & Bailey Circus performance where Dahl and his family were guests. "I was thinking I wasn't going to like him," Jackson told me at a coffee shop in Chicago's Ukrainian Village. "He was actually really nice. He mellowed [after he quit drinking]. Looking back, the emotional arc of Disco Demolition is that you had this outward moment of hate, highly focused onto a specific thing: disco music. After closer examination, it revealed itself to have racist and homophobic aspects. That may have not been Steve Dahl's mind frame at the time, but it came from somewhere. And it reverberated. Energy in, energy out."

When Dahl lost his job at JACK-FM in Chicago in December 2010, his wife was concerned. Joe Walsh's "Life's Been Good" was the final song he played before he signed off the air. "That was his life work, he was repudiated; time had passed him by," she reflected. "And that was at Christmas. He was devastated but resolved. He really likes communicating. He likes being the guy in the car. If there was a moment, I would think that's the moment he would have said, 'I'll just have one drink; it's Christmas'. But he is very determined.

"He realizes he is a better man."

the **LOOP** *Where Chicago Rocks FM98*
STEVE DAHL'S DISCO ARMY

№ 047

is a member in good standing in
THE INSANE COHO LIPS, the
Steve Dahl Disco Army, dedicated to
the eradication and elimination of the
dreaded musical disease known as
DISCO. The bearer of this card
devoutly pledges allegiance to
THE LOOP/FM98 and Steve Dahl,
the leaders in Chicago Rock 'n Roll!!

Steve Dahl promotional items

Steve Dahl at a promotional appearance for The Loop

3. BRIDGEPORT AND THE SOUTH SIDE

Bill Veeck loved incongruity. So it was a no-brainer to take maverick characters like Steve Dahl and Mike Veeck and introduce them to a neighborhood of convention and tradition.

To fully understand the dynamics of Disco Demolition you must understand Chicago in the late seventies. In 1979, the North Side and South Side were separate cities—much like they are today.

Walk around the two Chicago ballparks today. You will still see families sitting on porch steps around U.S. Cellular Field. Walking the streets around Wrigley Field, you have to watch out for frat boys playing hacky-sack. Even before Disco Demolition, Comiskey Park was the underdog. It was the perfect stage for Steve Dahl and Mike Veeck.

Steve Dahl arrived in Chicago from Detroit on February 21, 1978. He was hired to present "Steve Dahl's Rude Awakening" during the morning on WDAI-FM. Dahl was unaware of the characteristics of Chicago neighborhoods. And the South Side was warming up for Disco Demolition—with real rock 'n' roll concerts.

The World Series of Rock debuted with Aerosmith, Jeff Beck, and Ted Nugent on July 10, 1976. More than 62,000 fans poured into Comiskey Park. Two fires broke out in the upper grandstand and smoke covered the field. Over the next few years, Aerosmith, Foreigner, AC/DC, the Eagles, the Steve Miller Band, and Pablo Cruise would all play the Park.

Comiskey always smelled like the pigs, steers, and spent Kent cigarettes from the nearby Union Stockyards.

Bridgeport was waiting for something like Disco Demolition.

"I never thought of it that way," Dahl said. "Comiskey was a venue that was more wide open. The Beatles played there. I didn't know the neighborhoods when I got here. To me, the north, the south, the west, it was like *That '70s Show* everywhere. Chicago seemed similar to Detroit, it just seemed bigger with a thriving downtown. Already in those days Detroit was spotty. The music fans seemed the same. The weirdest thing is I never put that much thought into it.

"When I first got here they put me up downtown in a studio apartment, top floor. Swingles furniture. Jeff Finch was the news guy at WDAI, and he took me around for a week and showed me how everything worked around Chicago. I lived there for six months and went back to Detroit on weekends to see Janet. We got used to living apart all week, so all we did was fight all weekend."

"Steve fell in love with Chicago," Janet Dahl recalled. "But he came back to Detroit because I didn't want to leave. I owned a little condo and was committed to going to law school at night while I taught. Steve was so overwhelmed by living in Chicago. He was a lost soul, no friends. He was off at ten [a.m.] and eating pizza. [He] didn't have a chance to get traction [on air]. He was unhappy. We were living in Bolingbrook and I had no understanding of the South Side and the North Side. I always called both ballparks 'Friendly Confines.'"

Former Major League pitcher Ken Kravec knows both sides of Chicago. He pitched for the White Sox between 1975 and 1980 and for the Cubs in 1981 and 1982. As recent as 2012, Kravec was special assistant to the Cubs' general manager.

"I loved the old Comiskey," said Kravec. "It's a shame it couldn't be restored like Wrigley. You felt the fans were on top of you at Comiskey. It had so much history. They had let it go so long where it wasn't feasible to fix it up. I remember a lot of fights in the stands and the Sox security in their bright yellow shirts. There was something in that place. It seemed like there was a fight every night. Comiskey was a little rougher around the edges, for sure more than Wrigley. I remember fights going out on the field at Comiskey. You had that low wall near the lower deck. Every now and then somebody would tumble over that wall and you'd have to stop playing."

Dahl's former radio partner Garry Meier is a lifelong Chicagoan.

Meier was born in 1949 in the West Pullman neighborhood of Chicago, precisely 116th and Parnell—about eighty blocks south of Old Comiskey Park. The Meier family relocated to the southwest suburbs right before Meier enrolled at Tinley Park High School. He grew up a White Sox fan.

"I wasn't aware there was a whole lot to the North Side," Meier said over lunch at the Ralph Lauren restaurant on the near North Side.

"I was the oldest of six. I remember my father would load us up in the station wagon around the holidays. We'd come downtown, circle around the big Christmas tree, and go home. That was my visit to downtown Chicago. I saw the Prudential Building and go, 'Oh my God, its like Oz! Where is this city?' It was only fifteen, twenty miles from where we lived; we never came downtown. I was never into the North Side / South Side thing. The Cubs and Sox keep this divisive nature about the city. If we had two football teams, I guess we would have to pick one. That's the way the city has always been."

Former major league outfielder and pinch-hitter deluxe Thad Bosley can attest to that. He played on both sides of town; the White Sox from 1978 to '80 and the Cubs from 1983 to '86.

"Bridgeport was extremely difficult," Bosley said. "(White Sox general manager) Roland Hemond wanted me to live out in (the western suburb) Wheaton. Chet Lemon lived out in Wheaton. I would ride back and forth to the ballpark with Chet. After the ball game one night, I was driving and supposed to make the left to get on the Dan Ryan [Expressway]. I don't know what I was thinking, maybe there were fireworks or something, but I made a right. I ended up in Bridgeport. Some guys were throwing a football and all of a sudden they circled my car. Then, one of the guys said, 'No, that's Thad Bosley, he's okay.' I said, 'Hey man, I'm just trying to get to the freeway.' The guy said to me, 'Thad, people like you can't be here at nighttime. If these guys don't know you they will hurt you.' Then he showed me how to get out of there. That was a culture shock for me. I was like, 'Whoa, this is a few blocks away from the ballpark.'"

Poet and Disco Demolition vendor Bob Chicoine was born in 1951 and raised in the Auburn Gresham section of Chicago. "Disco Demolition was a South Side thing," Chicoine declared. "The South Side was in decline. Factories were closing. I grew up on the South Side and you grew up trying to be tough, although we're not as tough as we are now. We had brass knuckles and bicycle chains and that was it. Tough guys don't dance. And one thing about disco is that you danced with the girl. You weren't by any means graceful. When you're that age you define yourself by what you're opposed to as much as what you're for. There wasn't a war to oppose. There wasn't a lot of options. Disco was an obvious thing.

"Mike Veeck once said that this was their Woodstock, and it was true. There were all these cries of revelry and triumph, like 'We have taken over something.' We didn't take over the dean's office, but we took over our ballpark. That sense was all throughout the Southwest Side."

Acclaimed Chicago chef Kevin Hickey is a fifth generation Bridgeport resident. He was born in 1969 at Michael Reese Hospital. With Rockit Ranch Productions, Hickey opened the The Duck Inn in December 2014 in a former tavern and general store in Bridgeport. The pre-Prohibition trap door of the old Gem Bar Lounge still exists behind the bar. Gem Bar bowling trophies in the window date back to the 1960s.

"My family started on Archer Avenue with a horse and buggy business that morphed into the funeral business," Hickey said during an interview at the Duck Inn bar in the summer of 2015. His great-great-grandfather opened the J.J. Hickey Funeral Home, one of the first funeral homes in Chicago. His great-great grandfather died during the Depression.

"He had six kids and my great grandmother lost the business," Hickey said. "She didn't have a funeral director license. They owned a little piece of property at 35th and Ashland. The only thing she knew how to do was cook. She opened a diner and called it The Duck Inn. She ran it for several years and was successful enough to put my grandfather through mortuary school. She bought the business back and he built it up." The business was left to Hickey's father and mother who went on to open funeral homes in Logan Square and suburban Palos Hills. "Then they got divorced and it all went to hell," Hickey said.

After the divorce, Hickey's father stayed in Bridgeport and his mother moved north to the Gold Coast, which may have well been the opposite end of the world. "I lived in the Gold Coast from the time I was twelve until I went to college," Hickey said. "But I was back and forth, so I had interesting perspectives on the city. And going to De La Salle was very South Side and sports oriented, an 'all boys' kind of attitude. The teachers were either coaches or Christian brothers. It was no fun at all. For an entire year my English teacher did not call me by my name. He called me 'North Side F-word', the homophobic 'F' word. That was my name because I didn't live in the neighborhood."

Hickey spent his summers and school breaks in Bridgeport while attending University of Wisconsin. Between 1991 and 2004, he lived in Los Angeles, San Francisco, Dublin, Ireland, London, Paris, and Atlanta. He now lives in Bridgeport with his wife Javalen and son Declan.

Hickey was just ten years old when he attended Disco Demolition.

He brought the soundtrack to *Saturday Night Fever* to gain admission to the park. He liked baseball, he loved the Comiskey hot dogs, and he was a regular Dahl listener.

"Steve Dahl struck a chord with me when I was a kid," Hickey said. "I've always been obsessed with music. There were a lot of disco albums around the house with my mom and my sister. I was getting into punk, so I had a lot of Police and The Clash. My friends and I hated disco. It may have started out Latin-American based, but by 1979 everybody was listening to it. You felt you weren't pretty enough or skinny enough to fit into it. I was a chubby kid. I remember Steve saying the reason he hated disco so much was because he couldn't buy a three-piece white suit off the rack. That stuck with me because I couldn't, either. There was no Internet. We had three television channels and we had the radio on all the time.

"Bridgeport has changed so much since that time. It was very multi-generational in 1979. In the less-than mile walk from my house to Comiskey I knew who lived in every other house. Everybody knew who I was."

Kevin Hickey

Hickey referenced the 2008 Will Ferrell comedy *Semi-Pro*. "Comiskey felt like that movie," he said. "There were all these promotions going on to get people in the park and have fun. It was almost like a minor league team in a small town, and the whole town was centered around it. Comiskey was very much interwoven into the community of Bridgeport. We all went all the time. It's not the same. People started to leave in the 1980s and '90s."

"Bridgeport started in this area, at the end of [Eleanor] street with the bridge that went over to Ashland. It was a foot bridge and they used to bring barges in to go to the stockyards. They would portage on the bridge and that's how Bridgeport was named."

Bridgeport was originally named Hardscrabble, partly because Irish-American canal workers of the 1830s were paid for working on the Illinois and Michigan Canal with land deeds. The neighborhood has been considered an Irish-American island due to the Daley imprint, but in fact one of the most diverse neighborhoods in Chicago, with high populations of Chinese-Americans, Hispanics, Lithuanians, and Poles.

In 1972, North Siders Jerry Mickelson and Arny Granat founded Jam Productions—one of the largest independent concert promoters in America, producing more than 800 concerts in all fifty states, including the rock concerts at Comiskey Park.

Mickelson was on hand for Disco Demolition assisting Bill Veeck. The Disco Demolition disaster didn't stop Jam. Undeterred by the disaster of Disco Demolition, Jam booked Journey, Santana, Thin Lizzy, and Eddie Money as part of the August 5, 1979 "Loop's Day in the Park." More than 65,000 people attended, according to Mickelson's figures.

The Chicago White Sox and Jam Productions first partnered for a July 10, 1976 Aerosmith concert at Comiskey Park. In August 1978 Aerosmith returned to Comiskey. Competing promoters Celebration Productions had success with its 1976 "World Series of Rock" concerts, partnering with radio station WDAI to present Pink Floyd, Ted Nugent, and Emerson, Lake and Palmer at Soldier Field.

"At Comiskey we also did AC/DC, Cheap Trick, Journey," Mike Veeck said. "They were tremendous shows. The real disaster is the DC 10 that went down at O'Hare [Airport]. I put a guy on that flight who was the producer of Toronto Jam. We had a deal to do a two-day festival at Comiskey Park."

Flight 191 crashed on May 25, 1979—just a month before Disco Demolition.

Promoter Lenny Stogel was on the flight. He had been negotiating with Veeck to re-create a "Chicago Jam" similar to the 1978 "Canada Jam" that drew 110,000 people outside of Toronto. Stogel had previously managed the Cowsills singing group and steered the solo careers of Monkees' hit songwriters Tommy Boyce and Bobby Hart. Besides producing "Canada Jam" and "California Jam" (in 1974 and 1978 at the Ontario Motor Speedway), Stogel and his television partner Sanford Feldman produced the 1973 Evel Knievel Snake River Canyon Jump for ABC's *Wide World of Sports*. Stogel was traveling from Chicago to California to produce "California Jam III," which was cancelled.

"I had Tom Sulek, our resident [Comiskey] artist drive him to O'Hare," Veeck said. "The flight was down in twenty-two seconds. I brought Jerry [Mickelson] in when I panicked. I said, 'We're in a terrible world of hurt. I never should have done this thing without you guys.' When the producer of the show dies, (surviving partner) Feldman goes on with the deal. It's a two-day event with the Beach Boys, Rush, Blondie, and fifteen other acts. It tanked. It rained both days. No one was there. It was a disaster.

"There was nobody on the infield. The promoters needed people on the field there because it looked empty. They never cared about our ballpark, they only cared about how it looked on television. So he took the snow fence down. We had our security guys fighting the Toronto security guys. That's really what ruined the field, not Disco Demolition.

"Disco was July 12. That was August 18 and 19, 1979."

This would never happen at Wrigley Field.

"South Side rock 'n' roll had Rick Saucedo, Styx, obviously, Rufus and Chaka Khan," said Mickelson, who grew up in the far North Side neighborhood of Rogers Park. "The South Side was always different than the North Side. I don't know if the backlash against disco was a North Side/South Side thing. Dahl was the most vocal about how disco sucked. I was on the field. I don't think it was racist or homophobic. I remember people winging records at him as he was going around the field. You could tell the crowd was amped up."

"When we did our first show in 1976, Bill Veeck made us buy two season tickets as part of being allowed to do shows there," Mickelson said with a laugh. "So we've had those same seats basically since 1976. Bill Veeck was a promoter. He had the shower in center field where you could cool off. He had a barber out in the outfield. They were always looking for something different."

Legendary White Sox groundskeeper Roger Bossard worked with his father Gene Bossard during the 1979 season.

"Now they've got flooring [over the field]," Bossard said during an interview in his office at U.S. Cellular Field. "Concerts are still bad, but you can get away with it. In 1979 we hardly had drainage. The soil cavity structure was pure clay. Remember, Comiskey was a field from the 1930s. Now I have two miles of drainage here, and I put over three miles of drainage at Wrigley Field. The car in 1979 wasn't like the car now. I remember Bill [Veeck] telling me, 'You know Roger, it is called 'Veeck's Hex.' Whenever we had a concert, it rained. It was crazy. In 1979 I took forty-eight tons of drying compound and put it in right field just to dry it up. If that happened today, the players wouldn't play. But back in the day, the player's union wasn't that strong."

Jam and Veeck created the popular Bob Dylan/Willie Nelson tours of Minor League Baseball parks, which included a 2004 stop at the Baseball Hall of Fame and Museum in Cooperstown, New York. Mickelson said, "I looked at Disco Demolition as the most successful promotion Mike or anybody else has ever done."

In 1997, Veeck and Jam produced a concert and baseball game at Midway Field, the former home of the independent league St. Paul Saints, with Bob Dylan, singer-songwriter Ani DiFranco, and honky tonk band BR5-49. The show drew more than 11,000 fans to the ballpark. In 2004, Jam met with Dylan's camp and crafted a tour of twenty-two, Veeck-owned Minor League Baseball stadiums, including stops in Charleston, South Carolina, Brockton, Massachusetts, and Hudson Valley, New York.

As the Comiskey concerts were being produced, the now defunct Celebration Flipside was producing the "Super Bowl of Rock" at Soldier Field along Lake Michigan on the near South Side. 1979 The Loop General Sales Manager Jeff Schwartz said, "Comiskey was great for everything. I worked on 'The World Series of Rock'. I remember tying in Just Pants (the chain store) where you take your Molly Hatchett ticket and redeem it at any Just Pants location for a free Loop shirt. You wear the Loop shirt, wash it once, and all your clothes get black.

Chicago artist and author Tony Fitzpatrick was nineteen years old when he attended Disco Demoliton. He called Comiskey Park "a cultural station" and he still calls U.S. Cellular Field "Comiskey Park."

"The difference between the North and South Side is night and day," Fitzpatrick said during a conversation in his Northwest Side studio. "South of Madison Street, the chances are better the people work in the trades or work for the city. The North Side was a community of professionals, doctors, and lawyers. One of the big appeals for being a White Sox fan is that it was a team for working people. My uncles, cousins—it was always a big deal when they got tickets for the Sox because the Sox used to have twi-night double-headers! The White Sox weren't just a baseball team. They were a cultural station."

Of course, Disco Demolition was scheduled to be a twi-night double-header. Fitzpatrick said he attended dozens of White Sox games in 1979. "In a way, it was the only place for me to go," said Fitzpatrick, who grew up in the western suburb of Lombard. "As kids we knew there was a distinctive difference between Comiskey Park and Wrigley Field.

"Sox fans love the game. And the White Sox were pretty lousy my whole life until 2005. But there were years they threatened, like 1983, where I had to toss a coin to go to treatment for alcoholism or go to one more Sox game because they were winning ugly. Fortunately for everyone, I went into treatment. October 5, 1983 was my last drink."

White Sox fan Joe Bryl is the longest tenured club DJ in Chicago. He started at the Club 950 (AKA The Lucky Number) in 1981 and danced his way through the Lizard Lounge, Limelight, Funky Buddha Lounge, and Sonotheque, just to name a few. In 2015 he became musical director and general manager of the popular Maria's Packaged Goods & Community Bar, just four blocks away from the site of Comiskey Park.

Bryl was born in 1954 and grew up in the Back of the Yards neighborhood near the old Union Stockyards. His aunt Rose Ziemba ran a shot and beer joint at 47th and Racine, across the street from the stockyards. Bryl lives in the same house he grew up in.

Bryl has vivid memories of his father Joseph snagging Comiskey Park "box seat" tickets from Ready Metal Manufacturing, where he worked as a production control manager. "The box seats were on the second tier," Bryl said during a conversation at the Bridgeport Restaurant. "The seats were between (announcers) Harry Caray, Jimmy Piersall, and (White Sox organist) Nancy Faust. It was an open area. You would look to one side and see Harry and Jimmy doing their shtick. Nancy was in a booth that was open to the public. Everything was accessible. You were closer to the park. You could get lost in your own world. Not like nowadays."

Bryl was sitting next to his longtime friend and cultural comrade Rick Wojcik, owner of the internationally known Dusty Groove record store and mail order business located in the Ukrainian Village neighborhood of Chicago. Wojcik explained, "In the late 1970s there weren't the venues, there wasn't the ability to control it, these sports arenas were not built with that understanding. Disco Demolition happened at the same time the people were killed at The Who concert (December 3, 1979 at Riverfront Coliseum in Cincinnati, Ohio). The Amphitheater concerts were basically fire traps. There were so many things going at Comiskey. They did a lot of rock shows there."

Comiskey's neighboring International Amphitheater (capacity 9,000) was built in 1934 to host the International Livestock Exhibition. The old barn with lousy acoustics hosted the Beatles on August 12, 1966—the first show of their final tour. The 1979 anti-disco lineup included UFO and Judas Priest (May 1), Cheap Trick (June 16) and The Who (December 8). The hard rock band Rush cultivated its Chicago audience at the Amphitheater with home stands (April 3–6 1980, February 26–March 1, 1981). It is not a stretch to suggest that many of the fans of the 1979 Amphitheater rock concerts were also young White Sox fans. The rap group 2 Live Crew headlined the final concert at the Amphitheater in 1990 before it closed in 1999.

Dahl recalled, "We did a one-year anniversary for Disco Demolition at the Amphitheater. We were opening for Foghat. I had a mannequin I dressed up like Donna Summer. I broke it but I didn't know it was made out of glass. There was glass all over the stage. During 'Do Ya' Think I'm Disco' I went down on my knees for the rock 'n' roll part. I cut my knees and had to get stitches. When I went to the first aid room at the Amphitheater, I took my [general's] coat off. And somebody stole it."

In September 1972, the LA Thunderbirds were scheduled to meet the Midwest Pioneers in a roller derby match at the International Amphitheater. The venue was not available because of a livestock show. The promoters looked to Comiskey Park. The roller derby match drew 50,112 fans.

"Comiskey Park was very different than Wrigley Field in the late 1970s," said *Chicago Tribune* baseball writer Paul Sullivan, a native of the southern suburb Homewood. "You didn't want to stray outside the neighborhood, even to park three or four blocks away to get a free parking spot. Also to be careful when you're inside. It was such a drinking crowd. I once saw a guy at Comiskey who was so drunk he started peeing in his seat. I was like, 'What the fuck?' When I would go with my friends we went on expeditions through the whole park: the upper deck, the picnic area underneath the left field stands where you could harass the left fielder. I hung around center field a lot.

"To me, it wasn't just going to the game. It was an adventure."

Styx co-founder and composer Dennis DeYoung grew up during the late 1950s in the Roseland community, about sixty city blocks south of Bridgeport. "It was like *Happy Days*," he said during a conversation in his southwest suburban home. "We lived in a frame two flat on 101st Place. My grandparents lived downstairs. My parents owned the top half, they owned the bottom. My uncle lived downstairs. He was four years older than me. We didn't have a lot. We had what we needed. We felt like we were part of the great middle class of America.

"In that area in the late 1950s and early 1960s—and remember, this is before all the public unrest went on—the black community was on the other side of 99th Street. That was the dividing line. The families that lived there were a little bit economically higher than the white folks where I lived. Nice houses. Ernie Banks lived there, for goodness sake. Those kids had solid family structures. I never felt ostracized. I got along great with everybody. It was a good time. My recollection is maybe there were no more than twenty white kids left in my graduation class at Harlan High School. And it all was good, the black kids and the white kids. After 1965, things seemed to get dodgy.

"My parents had a big old Zenith Victrola. Seventy-eights. "Hit Parade" music. I played the accordion. This was before rock music, mind you. I joined the RCA Record club through the Chicago American, a working class newspaper. It was so broad. I was a sponge. I listened to melody, melody, and melody."

Schaller's Original Pump has always been in harmony with the South Side. The bar and diner has the second or third oldest liquor license in Chicago, according to fourth-generation owner Jay Schaller. The tavern opened in 1881 and got its name from the Ambrosia Nectar Brewing Co. that used to be in the current parking lot. Ambrosia pumped brew directly from the vat into the tavern's tappers during Prohibition.

The Pump has been across the street from the 11th Ward Democratic headquarters for more than sixty years. Former Mayor Richard J. Daley held countless election parties at the Pump. The mayor was a staunch White Sox fan, refusing to visit Wrigley Field, even on the invitation of the beloved Cubs Hall of Famer Ernie Banks. His son, Richard M. Daley (Chicago mayor 1989-2011) spent his twenty-first birthday at Schaller's.

The Union Stockyards were just a few blocks south of Schaller's Pump, encompassing 360 acres between 39th Street and 43rd Street. The stockyards opened in 1865; they were a city within a city. On a clear windy day, residents could smell bacon and ham. The goat that led the lambs up the ramp to the killing floor had a name—Judas. The stockyards had its own restaurant, radio station, and newspaper. Bubbly Creek ran through the yards, but Bubbly Creek is dried up now.

When the Stockyards closed in 1971, the White Sox lost a significant fan base of blue collar workers. Steve Trout is one of a few Major League Baseball players who were raised in Chicago and played for both the White Sox (1978–1982, including the Disco Demolition team) and the Cubs (1983–1987). During the last week of the 2014 baseball season, Trout walked into Schaller's Pump. He sat down next to Jack Schaller, now ninety, at a rear table. George "Harvey" Schaller, Jack's grandfather, was a German immigrant who opened the tavern.

"The South Side bleeds the team's color." Trout said. "The South Side demands a winner. If it was reversed, they would have a hard time getting anybody in Wrigley Field. On the South Side that blue collar dollar is deep in the pocket. It will come out when it has some value to it. I don't think they appreciate it anymore, but in a way they do. They want it to go further and further, [that's] when they walk out a little happier. "I have a unique view on the North Side and South Side. Comiskey Park was my playground as a boy. My Dad (former Detroit pitcher Paul "Dizzy" Trout) was working public relations for Bill Veeck. Dad's office was near Bill Veeck's office. Often Bill would say, 'Diz, you're going to be speaking in Decatur or Iowa, take Mike with you.'"

Trout leaned in to Schaller's good ear. He raised his voice and said, "We moved into a nun's convent in South Holland, Illinois. They asked Dad if he was Catholic. I had nine brothers and sisters. He said, 'No, just a passionate Protestant.' Dad took out the crosses in the hallways. There was a praying altar downstairs where we put our stereo set. He brought in a pool table and a keg of beer. Bill Veeck's picture. That would become our hanging out room.

"Dad would come home with the White Sox grounds crew and throw horseshoes until three in the morning. They'd barbecue because they got done with work at eleven o'clock. They'd get up, start work at eleven o' clock, get the field ready. They were real good people. Remember Gene Bossard?"

Schaller took a sip from his glass of ginger ale. He had not had a drop of alcohol in twenty-five years. He remembered Bossard. He also recalled Dizzy Trout coming to his bar with Bill Veeck.

Trout continued, "Gene's son (Roger) is still doing the grounds crew. He lived down the street. He was a good pool player but Dad beat him most of the time. Have you ever had a pool table in this joint?" Schaller said, "In the back."

Trout smiled and said, "I bet you saw some heavy games going on in there. Did you have any live music in here?"

According to Schaller, the Pump featured a Lithuanian accordion player for thirty years on Friday and Saturday nights. He played near the north end of the long wooden bar. "I liked Frank Sinatra," said Schaller. "This neighborhood has changed for the better. I was behind the bar on Disco Demolition. We had a good crowd but I didn't like it. I like the music of the 1940s, Tommy Dorsey and Glenn Miller. I have never served a tequila sunrise here."

Joe Shanahan is the owner of the popular North Side rock music clubs Smart Bar and Metro, each located a block from Wrigley Field. But Shanahan is from the south suburb of Evergreen Park and grew up in a White Sox household. His father John was a traveling salesman for a textile company, while his mother Vivian is a retired librarian who also worked at the Spiegel catalog company. John Shanahan died while Joe was attending Evergreen Park High School. John liked New Orleans jazz, Miles Davis and blues music. His older brother and sister liked the Beatles, Motown and the Rolling Stones. Shanahan said, "The first record I bought was the Rolling Stones' *Get Off My Cloud*."

He was twenty-two years old the summer of 1979.

"I could see the South Side kids I grew up with on the television running on the field," Shanahan said over a cup of tea at a North Side Greek diner. "Those were the douchebags I ran away from in high school. And they were burning records. I thought, 'Didn't you all read [Ray] Bradbury? Burning books? Burning records? This has the feeling of a really bad cloud. And why is it coming out of Chicago? And why is music of any kind, whether I like it or not, being destroyed for some radio promotion or some baseball promotion? It gave license for people to not be in the modern world. And Steve Dahl as the 'general' of that was racist, culturally-unbalanced, and a step back in saying 'White. Rock. Rules.' It didn't. We took that back. There was a hybrid of punk and hybrid of disco and we evolved it."

Steve Dahl at a promotional appearance for The Loop

Steve Dahl meeting fans before the first game of the double-header

4. THE 1979 CHICAGO WHITE SOX

If the White Sox had a decent team in 1979, Disco Demolition likely never would have happened. Get your pencils and scorecards ready:

The eightieth campaign in franchise history began on an inauspicious note with Donald Eulon Kessinger as player-manager. Kessinger was definitely counter to Comiskey's nocturnal culture: He was a former star shortstop for the Chicago Cubs, and he was a gentle and deeply religious soul from Arkansas.

On August 2, 1979, Kessinger retired as a player-manager, leaving behind a 46-60 record. "Kess" was replaced by coach and future Hall of Famer Tony La Russa.

"I think Bill Veeck was fascinated with my law degree," La Russa said during a 2015 spring training interview in Scottsdale, Arizona. "That's why I got the shot. They scouted me in winter ball in the Dominican and in Iowa (the Class AAA Oaks, where La Russa was managing on July 12, 1979). We finished 27-27 and I said, 'Will you hire me for the next year?' He was impressed how I loved the game and wanted to learn it. We were just together for those fifty-four games but he took me up to that Bard's Room and it was like going to graduate school every night. Those conservations with scouts and managers. Oh, my. And I would just sit and listen and learn. Bill and Mary Frances treated me like family. But I missed Disco Demolition.

"I wasn't a big disco fan."

The Kessinger/La Russa regime didn't have a lot of offense to work with, and the team finished in fifth place with a 73-87 record. Outfielder Chet Lemon led the White Sox with seventeen homeruns and a .318 average. Opening Day pitcher Ken Kravec went 15-13 with a 3.74 ERA.

"It wasn't a very good team," said Mike Veeck. "Don Kessinger would always resign for the good of the club. He would come in and offer himself all the time. Dad almost got to expect it, and one day he accepted, which shocked Kessinger."

In modest tones, Kravec recalled, "I probably had a lot to do with it, but when I played we weren't very competitive. I opened up the 1979 season on the road and at home. I don't know if we thought we had enough to go to the World Series, but we thought we'd be more than competitive. We had pitching: (the late Frankie) Barrios, (Ross) Baumgarten, Trout, myself, Farmer in the bullpen. But you never know how things will fall into place."

Just ask Steve Dahl and Mike Veeck.

"We had the good year in 1977 (The South Side Hit Men) and competed late until the season," Kravec continued. "We still won ninety games and finished third. It seemed like there was more energy at Comiskey than at Wrigley at that time. The 'Wrigley Field Experience' hadn't evolved yet. The fans seemed to be more into the game at Comiskey."

Former Styx frontman Dennis DeYoung is a White Sox fan dating back to the early 1960s. "I hated the White Sox then," he said. "The thing that pissed me off the most about Disco Demolition is that they didn't blow up those uniforms. Here's how bad it is. As a White Sox fan in 1979, in protest, on tour, I wore a Cubs jersey tailor made for me. As Yogi [Berra] used to say, you can look this up. If you're a White Sox fan, you don't like the Cubs. But I was the silent majority. Ralph Garr. Lamar Johnson. I hated the team, but [Bill] Veeck was trying to do anything to save them. He was a good guy, smart and funny."

DeYoung was a White Sox season ticket holder from 1984–1994. The baseball strike of 1994 robbed the heart of many White Sox fans, and DeYoung was one of them.

"The Sox had a chance to win the World Series," he said. "They called me and asked why I had not sent in my money for the coming year. I told them, 'Settle the strike and I'll send it.' They didn't and I didn't. Tony LaRussa and I discussed this at the time and he understood. Once we were out to eat with Jerry Reinsdorf (owner of the White Sox after Veeck) and Tony had me tell Jerry my feeling about the strike. I did it as a fan of baseball and pulled no punches. The strike destroyed the illusion. Jerry understood, having heard this stuff before. Jerry is a good guy. Hell, he paid for dinner."

The oddballs of the 1979 White Sox team included third baseman Jim Morrison (as in "Light My Fire"), musician/out-fielder Thad Bosley (who went on to play for the Cubs), and outfielder Rusty Torres. Torres was the only man in Major League Baseball to play in the three forfeited games of the 1970s: He was the starting right fielder in Disco Demolition; he was on second base for the Cleveland Indians on June, 4, 1974 when Indian fans stormed the field, inspired by "Ten Cent Beer Night" at old Municipal Stadium; and on the rainy afternoon of September 30, 1971, Torres was in the on deck

Ed Farmer

circle in the ninth inning of the Washington Senators' final game in D.C. Hooligans stormed the field and the game was forfeited to the New York Yankees. Just like the patio seats at Comiskey Park's Disco Demolition, fans tore up the seats at Robert F. Kennedy Stadium.

(In December, 2014 Torres was sentenced to three years in prison for sexually abusing an eight-year-old girl during a baseball practice in the Long Island town of Oyster Bay where he worked as a youth baseball coach. Torres was unavailable for comment.)

Besides Kravec, the 1979 pitching staff included current White Sox announcer Ed Farmer (3-7, 2.43 ERA) and Steve Trout (11-8, 3.89). As much as Comiskey and Disco Demolition may not have made sense to the straight-laced Kessinger, this whole thing was right in Trout's left handed wheelhouse.

His father Paul (nickname "Dizzy") pitched for the Detroit Tigers between 1940 and 1953.

Steve "Rainbow" Trout was born in Detroit the summer of 1957, and in 1965, moved with his family to the Chicago south suburb South Holland.

Trout pitched the night before Disco Demolition. Before the first game of the double-header, he was interviewed by Sox announcer Harry Caray about his performance. "I noticed the big green doors opened up in center field," Trout said. "Where the relief pitchers came in. And sure enough, it's Steve Dahl and two hot looking girls with him. As he approached our dugout, Harry noticed the girls more than anyone else. He left me in the middle of a question and goes right over to Dahl and says, 'Hey girls, are you also here for the disco party?' The stands were just filling up. I didn't realize there would be so many metal fans in silver and black. It was anti-disco all right, but I remember they were out of beer by the fifth inning of the first game. Bill Veeck used to say, 'When you're out of beer, you're out of Bill,' and we'd go off to Miller's Pub until four in the morning. It was a hot night."

After his 1978 rookie season with the White Sox, Trout took a winter job to call season ticket holders.

American League Standings, July 13, 1979—the day after the White Sox forfeited game two of Disco Demolition to the Detroit Tigers:

Western Division
California - 52-38 - (GB)
Texas - 50-38 - 1
Minnesota - 46-40 - 4
Kansas City - 43-45 - 8
Chicago White Sox - 40-47 - 10 1/2
Seattle - 39-52 - 13 1/2
Oakland - 25-66 - 27 1/2
Eastern Division
Baltimore - 57-30 (GB)
Boston - 53-32 - 3
Milwaukee - 51-38 - 7
New York - 49-40 - 9
Detroit - 42-44 - 14 1/2
Cleveland - 42-45 - 15
Toronto - 28-62 - 30 1/2

Trout laughed and recalled, "I'd say, 'This is Steve Trout, would you like to renew your season tickets?' They'd say, 'Not if you're pitching next year.' I also had a winter job that year as Santa Claus at Sears & Roebuck in the River Oaks Mall on the the South Side. I did it for four weeks. They paid me better than the White Sox!"

Dahl has been a White Sox season ticket holder since the early 1990s.

"When I first came to town I tried to be a Cubs fan because I grew up in LA. National League and all that," he said. "I became a Sox fan later. I was persona non grata there for a while and then (former *Daily Herald* sportswriter and Sox media manager) Rob Gallas reached out to me. He was the one who kind of made [Disco Demolition] part of Sox lore. He embraced it rather than try to hide it. That's really what got me as a White Sox fan. I was part of the team's history and felt connected to it."

The 1979 White Sox drew only 1,280,762 fans to Comiskey—an average of 16,211 a game, good for tenth in the fourteen team American League. Games were broadcast on WSNS Channel 44. The famous 1977 South Side Hit Men drew 1,657,135 (average 20,458 a game) which was fifth best in the American League just two years earlier. Attendance tumbled hard in 1978 and early 1979. Attendance on the night before Disco Demolition was a paltry 15,520. Something had to be done.

Steve Dahl signs autographs before the first game of the double-header

Dennis DeYoung

5. CHICAGO ROCK IN A DISCO WORLD

Nothing rocks like a Chicago South Sider, a place where hard blues meets amped up attitude.

Chicago carries a legacy of muscular rock 'n' roll.

The American Breed had late 1960s national hits like "Bend Me, Shape Me" and "Step Out of Your Mind" before evolving into Rufus. And Rufus recruited Hyde Park native Chaka Khan. (The American Breed resurfaced in time for the 2005 White Sox World Championship, releasing the single "Rock With The Sox.") Maurice White and Earth, Wind and Fire emerged in 1969 from the Chess Records recording studio in the South Loop.

Styx was formed in the early 1960s in the far South Side neighborhood of Roseland when brothers Chuck (guitar) and John Panozzo (drums) got together with vocalist-keyboardist Dennis DeYoung. Styx was riding high the summer of 1979 with *Cornerstone*, its third of four triple platinum albums. Their 1980 tour was seen by 1.5 million fans—at the time, the most people ever to see an American rock band.

"The South Side was a real rock 'n' roll place," said Sox announcer Ed Farmer, who, like Joe Shanahan and the late Ray Manzarek, guitarist of The Doors, grew up in the south suburb of Evergreen Park. "When I played I listened to Styx. Chicago. The Spinners, Marvin Gaye, and Tammi Terrell. The Four Seasons. Steve Trout? He listened to things that were being sent from another planet."

Former outfielder Thad Bosley was a teammate of Trout's on the 1979 White Sox and the 1984 Cubs—the National League Eastern Division champions.

"We listened to a lot of different styles of music," Bosley said. "Steve Trout and I talked music all the time. Same with (1979 White Sox players) Lamar Johnson, Ralph Garr and Chet [Lemon]. When I first came to Chicago they called me a white boy because I listened to Crosby, Stills, Nash and Young and James Taylor. I grew up in a surfing town in Oceanside, California. So I had The Supremes, Earth, Wind and Fire, and Stevie Wonder—but I also had America and Bread. They're like, 'Dude . . .' But I like soft. Through my mom and dad I heard everything from traditional gospel to jazz. So when [pop] songs would come on the radio they'd go, 'Dude, how did you know that song?' I'd say I grew up on it.

"I was pretty quiet about my music in 1979. I've never been a fan of disco. I felt it was for the most part revenue generated. I'm not saying there weren't talented people in disco, obviously Donna Summer comes to mind, but it didn't seem like you had to do much other than get 104 beats per minute and re-peat. It seemed like it was focusing on a club versus really having to sit down and construct a song. I can appreciate elements of disco just like I can appreciate playing in the National and American leagues. But I'm a traditional baseball guy."

During the summer of 1979, Styx was big in the White Sox club house, according to Farmer and Trout. Trout recalled, "La Russa had a friendship with Dennis DeYoung. And Styx was in Frankfort, not far from the South Side. I was playing a lot of Santana. There was always Yes being played. I got to hang out with (Yes drummer) Alan White for a while. Yes was one of my favorite bands of the 1970s and '80s. I listened to a lot of Sly & the Family Stone. I would listen to soul music on my dad's stereo. When we lived in De-troit I got a chance to visit Hitsville, U.S.A. When I came to Chicago I'd go to [the original] Checkerboard Lounge (on 43rd Street on the South Side).

"I don't remember any disco music in the club house. For sure Dennis DeYoung. Tony (La Russa) had him around a lot. There were probably three boom boxes going on simultaneously with music. It was a lively club house. Getaway day, a little more music. After a loss, not much."

La Russa said, "I've always loved classic rock. The true story is that when I got the job in 1979, for the last fifty-four games there was a rock station that had a midnight show with interviews, it was called Zero B.S. or something. So I did the interview. The Sox encouraged me to get out as much as I could because nobody knew who I was—probably a good thing. In between our interview, they played music. I named three or four bands, and one of them was Styx. The next day I was at the ballpark. They're always messing with you, but security called and said, 'Dennis DeYoung is here to see you.' I said, 'Why don't you just kiss my ass?' and hung up the phone because everybody was yelling at me for being on Zero B.S. And then there's a knock on the door and it is Dennis DeYoung. Turned out he is a season ticket holder and a friend of his was listening to the show. He introduced himself and we've been good friends ever since."

During an interview in his home in southwest suburban Chicago, DeYoung recalled, "My best friend Tom Short was listening to The Loop. This new White Sox manager (La Russa) was talking about his favorite bands. He said, 'Styx or Journey?' I said, '[Old school White Sox managers] Al López? Eddie Stanky?' I've never done anything like this in my life. I'm anti-social when it comes to the rock scene. I don't like it. I have a wife. The only appeal of the scene is if you want to do drugs and get laid by strangers, neither of which I'm going to do.

"But I went and got a [Styx] tour jacket. I drove to 35th and Shields. I went into the office and said, 'I came by to leave a tour jacket for Tony La Russa.' They asked who I was. I said, 'I'm Dennis DeYoung,' so she calls the clubhouse. The guard comes to take me into the clubhouse. The doors open and there's all these guys walking around with their dongs hanging out. The door opens to the manager's office and there's Tony in a sweatshirt, long johns and flip flops. He came out of the office and goes, 'Dennis DeYoung!' I went, 'Tony La Russa!' Just like that. So we went into his office. We talked for an hour and a half like we knew each other. My love of baseball, his love of music. All the time this other guy in the office is writing. He's doing a cover story on the White Sox for *Sports Illustrated*. I'm there. Guess what? I made *Sports Illustrated*—more important to me than *Rolling Stone*. Then we become friends. We hang. Because of that, I hung with Farmio (Ed Farmer), [pitcher Richard] Dotson, Trout. I was there all the time. It was like a dream. I took batting practice, I shagged fly balls at Comiskey Park. When I was eleven, if I had my choice of being Paul McCartney or (White Sox center fielder) Jim Landis, I would be Jim Landis."

La Russa includes Bruce Hornsby and Bruce Springsteen among his friends. At a concert in San Francisco in 2007, Hornsby adapted his song "Hooray for Tom" (with lyrics like, "Teach me long division / So I can figure out baseball stats / Batting average, fielding percentage and all that . . . ") and dedicated it to La Russa. "You get around entertainers and they want to talk sports," La Russa said. "You get around sports and they want to talk entertainment. I'm that way about books. I love people who write books."

Like Styx, Cheap Trick was at the top of its game in the summer of 1979. On July 4, 1979, the Rockford band co-headlined the Winnebago County Fair in a "homecoming" show at Texarkana Fairgrounds in Pecatonica, Illinois with AC/DC and Molly Hatchett. Steve Dahl and Teenage Radiation were the opening act. *Cheap Trick at Budokan* was released in February 1979, and it would become an iconic album.

Japanese fans embraced Cheap Trick on their maiden tour of Japan in 1978. The *Budokan* tracks were taken from that tour. The album went triple platinum in the United States. The breakout hit was "I Want You to Want Me," which turned out to be the biggest selling single in Cheap Trick's career.

"It was hard to get a record deal because of all the disco stuff," Cheap Trick guitarist Rick Nielsen said in a February 2015 interview in the heated patio of his home in Rockford, Illinois. "Donna Summer. Gloria Gaynor. We had no chance of doing anything, but we just did [music] we liked. It became a backlash to everything going on.

"I didn't hate all disco. I loved the Bee Gees, but I liked the older Bee Gees more. Their singing was great, plus [twins] Robin and Maurice [Gibb] were born on December 22, 1948, which is my birthday, too. But as time went by they kept changing their birthdays to 1950, '51, and Rolling Stone moved me to 1946. I'm old enough!"

Chaka Khan (Yvette Marie Stevens) is a feisty native of Chicago's South Side whose timeless music defies categorization. The ten-time Grammy winner's repertoire features jazz, rock, funk, soul, and pop music. Her biggest hits include 1973's "Tell Me Something Good," the Stevie Wonder composition recorded with the Chicago pop-rock outfit Rufus, and her solo dance tracks "I'm Every Woman" (1979) and "I Feel For You" (1985), both of which won Grammys for Best R&B Vocal Performance, Female.

"Disco didn't phase me," Khan said with a hearty laugh. "I didn't do any disco songs but my stuff ended up being played in clubs. I never once said, 'Let's do a disco song.' No one asked me to do a disco song. I recall being able to dance whether it was disco or not. My stuff was funky.

"I went to a few discos but it was never my thing to just go out and dance. I liked to go out and listen to bands, see jazz. I got blasted and went to a disco once in a while. I went to Faces [in Chicago] twice, maybe? I knew Donna Summer. I loved her work. Everything is music. We always come back to that same place in the end. No matter where the conversation starts, good music is good friggin' music. Period."

A decade after Disco Demolition, Khan emerged in the nascent house music scene when Warner Brothers released the double CD *Life is a Dance: The Remix Project* of Khan's recordings. It included Chicago house legend Frankie Knuckles' dance floor smash, a remix of the Rufus hit "Ain't Nobody."

At the time of Disco Demolition, Khan was recording her R&B album, *Naughty*, the second solo project of her career. "To me, those were my best recording days," she said in the winter of 2016. "I loved working with [producer] Arif Mardin. Whitney Houston and her mother were on that record. So was Luther Vandross. I explored a lot of stuff that was within me and Arif brought it out. He felt we could stretch my jazz aspects. He could challenge it without being fearful, which was great."

Khan was born and raised in Hyde Park and learned violin and flute in Catholic school and Kenwood Academy, where R&B artist R. Kelly would go to school. Her parents were research analysts at the University of Chicago. Khan paid her dues on pre-disco era Rush Street, singing hot and hard soul music with Baby Huey and the Babysitters and Shades of Life.

Rufus formed in 1970 and became one of the first interracial funk bands. "The first album I ever bought was Led Zeppelin's first album in high school," she said. "If you look at early Rufus, that's what we were doing."

By the time of Disco Demolition, Khan had left Chicago for a solo career.

"There were some other music riots in Chicago other than Disco Demolition, you know," she said with a laugh. "The Sly Stone uprising [at the Grant Park band shell]. I was there."

Chaka Khan

In July of 1970, the Chicago Park District sponsored a Sly & the Family Stone concert. Khan was backstage with the opening psychedelic rock band Fat Water and members of Rufus. A riot broke out, far more serious than Disco Demolition. More than ninety people were hurt and 148 fans were arrested in a crowd that was estimated at 40,000.

After Fat Water opened, Sly & the Family Stone were nowhere to be found.

"Sly was in a helicopter but the helicopter did not land," Khan told the *Chicago Sun-Times* in 2013. "When he saw the police let loose with the canine units, it was too late. Those were turbulent times. Those were my post-Panther days. I wasn't really surprised that happened."

The following day the *Sun-Times* reported, "Dozens of policemen were struck by showers of bottles and stones that were hurled repeatedly by the racially integrated mob [. . .] At one point [police] fired their revolvers to fend off a charge of thousands of demonstrators. Most of them pointed their guns above the youth's heads, but some held their weapons level."

An African shaman changed Yvette Marie Stevens' name to Chaka Adunne Aduffe Hodhari Karifi while she was a member of the Black Panthers. Each name denotes a guardian spirit. Chaka is the feminine pronunciation of Shaka Zulu, the warrior that denotes war, the color red, and the planet Mars. She became Chaka Khan after marrying Staple Singers bassist Hassan Khan in 1970.

"Violence in Chicago has been going on forever," Khan told me. "Chicago is a very progressive, artistic city; on the other hand it is extremely racist. 'Fragmented' is a good word for Chicago when it comes to social issues and boundary issues. I was very affected by that. But the city has so much to offer."

* * *

Mitch Michaels understands the lure of Chicago. He has been a Chicago rock jock since 1971. Born and raised in Cleveland, Ohio, his mother Shirley was a homemaker and his father Louis Salchow Myers was an executive with the American Greetings Corporation. Michaels came to Chicago to deejay for WGLD (102.7-FM), which broadcast from the fifth floor of the Oak Park Arms Hotel, a reconfigured senior citizen's home in Oak Park, Illinois.

In June 1972, Michaels became one of the original DJs at WXRT (93.1) FM, before going to WDAI in 1973, back to 'XRT in 1975, back to WDAI in September of 1976, down the dial to WKQK three months later, before finally landing at WLUP in March 1979—three months before Disco Demolition.

During a conversation in his home in the western suburb of Hinsdale, Michaels said, "A vibrant [rock] club scene started to build in the mid-1970s. You had Durty Nellie's [in Palatine, Illinois], Biddy Mulligan's [on the far North Side of Chicago], Thirsty Whale [hard rock near River Grove], Haymaker's [in Prospect Heights, Illinois]. People remember that vibrant time. You had Rocket North, which was just over the line in [Kenosha County] Wisconsin. You could drink beer at age eighteen there."

As disco grew in popularity, many club owners found it cheaper and easier to hire DJs instead of live bands. Disco DJs did not come with a demanding manager and road crew. Dusty Groove's Rick Wojcik said, "From a record company's perspective, disco was more cost effective than locking up a band in a studio for six months. Disco was riding on that older school where, 'We've got a bunch of session guys, we're going to bring them in for four hours, and we've got a hit. We can get a whole album done.' Chicago was much more of a working class city then. It's like the way Cleveland worked out for bands like Rush that never would have broken in New York or LA. You even saw that continue in the 1980s. Naked Raygun was such a working class band and those shows brought in blue collar kids from everywhere."

Cheap Trick left the Chicago area club scene in 1976 as disco was making inroads. "We started opening shows and recording," Nielsen said. "B' Ginnings was one of the last clubs we did."

B'Ginnings opened in 1974 near the Woodfield Mall in Schaumburg, Illinois. The club's principal owner was Danny Seraphine, at the time, the drummer for Chicago. The urban interior and murals reflected the band's roots in the Lincoln Park neighborhood of Chicago. "The show we played there was the most money we ever made playing clubs," Nielsen said. "And Tom Petty was the opening act for us. Then we got a record deal and made no money."

Haymaker's also featured the Bangles, Twisted Sister, and Sly Stone looking for a comeback. The club closed in 1984, during the aftermath of disco. Nielsen said, "We played Haymaker's all the time. We started there with no audience. I smashed the dropped ceiling out of that place a number of times. Joe Townsend was the owner. He went with us on our first trip to Japan. He was one of our bodyguards. Jim Sohns (lead singer of the Shadows of Knight) came to Haymaker's one time and I shoved him up into the ceiling. That was one of my trademarks."

There were no disco balls in the Haymaker's ceiling.

"The seventies were a weird time for music," said Michaels. "Think about the stuff that came out that year: *Led Zeppelin IV*, *Who's Next*, Rod Stewart's *Every Picture Tells a Story*, [The Doors'] *L.A. Woman*. For the next several years, it was like, 'What happened?'"

The Top Ten on the Billboard "Hot 100" charts ending July 21, 1979 were:

1. "Bad Girls," Donna Summer
2. "Ring My Bel," Anita Ward
3. "Hot Stuff," Donna Summer
4. "Good Times," Chic
5. "Makin It," David Naughton
6. "Boogie Wonderland," Earth, Wind and Fire with the Emotions
7. "I Want You To Want Me," Cheap Trick
8. "Shine a Little Love," Electric Light Orchestra
9. "Gold," John Stewart (formerly of the Kingston Trio)
10. "She Believes In Me," Kenny Rogers

Nielsen said, "I've heard that rock 'n' roll was dead ever since we started [in 1974], 'These guys will never last.' Not just us, but the Stones and the Beatles, 'They're over.' The only one that left in a hurry was the Dave Clark Five. You never heard from them after the first three or four years. And I know him. I had Thanksgiving dinner with [Dave Clark] last year in London. I hate to be a name dropper, but I'm Rick Nielsen from Rockford, Illinois.

"Even when I was growing up, the stuff I liked was usually what was not on the radio. Every Sunday night on K-ROCK in Little Rock, Arkansas, they played the top ten songs from England. I had a Volkswagen and I had to pull my car over because you could barely get the signal. You had to search for it. Rock is dead for the people it is dead for."

Garry Meier reflected on the summer of 1979: "You were thinking, 'Is this the wave that is going to completely suffocate rock 'n' roll?' Seems impossible to think about that now, but in those years, disco did push rock 'n' roll in the background. Because radio stations react to one moment. They started to play Donna Summer because they thought that was their key to success. They didn't give a shit about rock 'n' roll. They gave a shit about ratings and revenue. They'd play gospel and polka if they figured that would work. In the late 1970s and early '80s disco did dominate the radio."

"Before Steve and I connected, I was working all night at The Loop," Meier said. "And that was very much rock 'n' roll: Uriah Heep, The Who. I loved it. To get to a rock 'n' roll station was my dream. Throughout the 1970s, WDAI was my favorite radio station because it was rock and I liked the disc jockeys. But The Loop pushed back the surge of disco. We were the beach head. That's why The Loop became The Loop, the black T-shirts and all that. When Chicago Fest was on Navy Pier (1978–1983), the fever of rock 'n' roll was still alive.

"After Disco Demolition, it was Chicago Fest that kind of kept rock alive. Cheap Trick played that on those docks that were tied on the water. It was *raw*. Funky, Navy Pier rock 'n' roll, people walking around with plastic beer cups stacked after they drank them. Think about how sanitized Taste of Chicago is to that. There was an energy to Chicago Fest, our roots. 'Yeah, we're very blue collar.' There's no feeling now."

Disco had reached Japan in 1979 and 1980. Cheap Trick was all the rage, touring across the country. "Everything was on the radar," Nielsen said. "They like their domestic groups, too. They like the little girl stuff; it is so diverse there. But they love American rock 'n' roll. I love the Japanese; they were the first place that liked us as a group. Thank God we were good. We knew how to play because of playing Haymaker's and the Thirsty Whale. Our first big show in Chicago was in 1980 at Chicago Fest."

Although Yoko Ono singles like "Hold Me" and "Talking to the Universe" are contemporary dance hits, Nielsen did not recall much disco talk in the air during the 1980 sessions for *Double Fantasy*, the final album of John Lennon's career. The band's seminal mid-1970s work with Jack Douglas (as well as with Aerosmith and the New York Dolls) brought them into the Lennon camp. Nielsen and Cheap Trick drummer Bun E. Carlos played on an intense version of "I'm Losing You," as well as Ono's "I'm Moving On" in late night sessions at the Hit Factory in New York City.

"John Lennon was a recluse and wasn't doing anything," Nielsen said. "We got a call because of Jack Douglas who produced our first record and mixed the *Live at Budokan* record with Bun E. and I. I don't even know how much John knew about bringing in these guys from Cheap Trick. John walked in and looked at me and said, 'Oh, it's you!' I think he thought it was going to be Rick Nelson from Ozzie and Harriet, but he knew who I was. We talked about guitars and the Mellotron (a tape replay keyboard which the Beatles used on "Strawberry Fields Forever") because I was the first guy in the United States to have Mellotron. In 1980, disco was leaving and a lot of hair bands and keyboards started coming in.

Rick and Karen Nielsen

"We only did half of *Double Fantasy* with John because it was like, 'No one is going to ever hear this.' It came off a bit heavier than the stuff on the final release. It was hush-hush. The night before, we had played in Montreal. I got a call from my wife that we had Daxx (Nielsen's son and current drummer for Cheap Trick). The only reason I was not at the hospital like I was for my other three kids is because it was John Lennon. I had to be in New York. As far as I know, he wanted to go back on tour, and he wanted Cheap Trick to be his band."

Rick and Karen Nielsen were married in 1971. Their commitment has outlasted bubble gum, disco, and urban cowboy music. They never went to a disco club together. Karen looked across the room and said, "He always worked.

"And there's not many discos in Rockford."

James Michael Peterik, Jim, is a product of muscular, mid-century Berwyn, a nearby suburb of Chicago. There aren't many discos in Berwyn, either.

The son of an electrician and weekend VFW hall saxophone player, Peterik grew up listening to Johnny Cash, Elvis Presley, and other Sun Records artists out of Memphis, Tennessee. Peterik has always possessed an independent spirit, so it was not surprising to find him on an early fall afternoon in 2015 answering the door of his southwest suburban mansion with purple hair, purple tinted glasses, and a matching purple belt buckle.

In keeping with his individuality, he would form the rock band Survivor in the winter of 1977—the apex of the disco movement.

Survivor is best known for its number one single "Eye of the Tiger," which won a Grammy for Best Rock Performance by a Duo or Group with Vocal, garnered an Academy Award nomination, and was the theme song for the hit film *Rocky III*.

Peterik was a member of Survivor between 1978 and 1989, and again between 1993 and 1996. The band continues to perform without him.

"By 1978 Survivor was playing all the clubs in the area," said Peterik. "The Thirsty Whale, Studio One in Downers Grove. We used to pack that place." Studio One on West Ogden Avenue was a launching pad for bands like EYZ that would later appear on WLUP-FM compilation albums.

"We got our local following before we ever put out a record," Peterik recalled. "We played the Pointe East in Indiana, right over the border. Of course the Wisconsin clubs where you could drink when you were eighteen. Our first big deal shows were in 1980, '81, at 'Rock Around the Dock' at ChicagoFest."

On July 30, 1981, Survivor headlined "Rock Around the Dock" at Navy Pier. On July 31, 1981, Steve Dahl appeared as Elvis at "Rock on the Roof," at Navy Pier's ChicagoFest. "Those were rowdy times," Peterik said. "Dave Bickler was our singer. He went on to sing 'Eye of the Tiger,' the biggest song of our career. He had his beret on. At the time me and Frankie Sullivan were a good team. Dave was the cute kid, the Peter Frampton look alike. I was me. I wasn't the star quality."

Unlike many late 1970s rock bands, Survivor did not have trouble getting gigs as disco took over clubs and venues. "The most it affected us is that when we cut our first album we had a song called 'Whole Town's Talking,'" Peterik said. "We took it in a disco funk direction. Our fans asked, 'Why did you do that?' We pandered to the trend a bit, with the high hat beat. I know if I had any leanings towards disco, Frankie Sullivan would have stopped it. He was hard rock and I respected that. But disco didn't affect the gigs at all. As soon as the first (self-titled) record hit, we were out of the clubs and on tour with Jefferson Starship,

Kansas, Heart. We were doing the songs from that album, 'Somewhere in America' 'Rockin' Into the Night.'" (The bluesy "Rockin' Into the Night" was rejected by producer Ron Nevison, the engineer on Led Zeppelin's *Physical Graffiti*, and later became a hit for .38 Special.)

The album *Survivor* was recorded in the summer of 1979 at the Record Plant in Los Angeles as Disco Demolition was going down. Actress-model Kim Basinger appeared on the album cover, although Peterik never met her.

"Disco Demolition was a big deal," Peterik said. "It was Steve Dahl's 'Eye of the Tiger.' That was his claim

Jim Peterik

into the history books and I was all for that. I wasn't into the disco thing at all. I ignored it. In 1977 I did write and produce 'Gotta Dance to Keep From Crying' (not to be confused with the 1963 Miracles hit) for Samona Cooke, allegedly Sam Cooke's niece, for Epic Records. The flip side was a disco cover of the Bee Gees 'Subway.' But I wasn't at Disco Demolition.

"When things are overdone, there's a backlash. Not long after Disco Demolition everything with a synthesizer and disco beat was an anathema to rock fans. There were more rock fans than disco fans. We overtook the disco scene. That was something for Studio 54 in New York. That wasn't the heartland of the Midwest. To us it was a passing fad, which is what it became. When I do look back, I like some of it. 'Fly Robin Fly' (the 1975 hit by Silver Convention) is still one of my favorite tracks. The best—the archetypal 'Disco Inferno.' (The 1976 hit by the Trammps). I remember dancing to that with [my wife] Karen at Morton's downtown. They had a big room with the disco ball and they were blasting music. I found myself getting into it."

A small, silver guitar necklace hung around his neck, designed by Jeff Rutt of Fine Gold Jewelry in Hinsdale, Illinois. The links of the chain spell out "Eye of the Tiger," and "Vehicle"—Peterick's 1970 smash with the Ides of March. On the back of the chain, silver script honors Karen and their son Colin.

Peterik co-wrote the .38 Special hits "Hold On Loosely" (1981) and "Caught Up in You" (1982) with the band's guitarist Don Barnes. In 1981, Peterik wrote "Heavy Metal" with Sammy Hagar.

Rocky III filmmaker Sylvester Stallone originally wanted Queen's bombastic "Another One Bites the Dust," but he could not secure the rights. Survivor's manager Tony Scotti had told Stallone about the Chicago-based power rockers who played without ornamentation. Peterik explained, "Rock 'n' roll has a rebellious streak, and it certainly rebels against glitz and glamour and synthesized music. It has always been that way. The Scotti Brothers were great in that there was no meddling on disco. We just kept rocking." Before Survivor, Peterik rocked his way onto the charts with the Berwyn based band, Ides of March. They incorporated soulful horns in the style of Blood, Sweat and Tears and Chicago for hits like "Vehicle" and the 1964 breakout single "You Wouldn't Listen." The Ides also had a hit with the ballad "L.A. Goodbye." The Ides also played discotheques, the clubs whose names birthed the term "disco."

"The Ides of March played a number of discotheques," he said. "The Chevalla Phase 3 was a discotheque in St. Louis. We were ducks out of water, we were roots of rock with 'L.A. Goodbye' and 'Vehicle.'" Peterik said his Berwyn-Cicero roots leaned towards the South Side, but his father Jim was an avid Cubs fan. "I grew up a Cubs fan, and the early days of going to Cubs park with my folks is quite memorable," he said. "But now I'm both. The White Sox treat us well. We do the National Anthem quite a bit there and we do a seventies night where we actually do a set."

Dennis DeYoung declared, "Do you think any bands were afraid of the future of rock 'n' roll? Talk to me, I'm making the fucking records. Did any rock bands say they were afraid of disco? It did take up radio airplay time, but other than that, what did I care? Rock 'n' roll is dead. The internet killed rock 'n' roll. It's pop music now. What was the last great rock band? The Black Keys? I forgot. Who plays great rock music on the radio now? WXRT?"

The Metro's Joe Shanahan was tuning out rock music in the late 1970s. He said, "In 1979 I was also opposed to a lot of the rock music that was happening; 1977 was the Clash, the Ramones, Talking Heads, and Blondie. The whole CBGB's thing and the UK punk explosion. That's where my focus was. I was diametrically opposed to bad disco. Some of the UK stuff was rooted in reggae, which was important. The black and white was blurred, the gay-straight line was blurred as well.

"La Mere Vipere here in Chicago was a gay club that did a punk rock night, which then became a punk rock club. Taco and Mike Rivers at Soundstage Records were DJs and they were gay guys. And they had fantastic taste in music."

Chicago club DJ Joe Bryl's father was a cartoonist who worked for the Polish Daily Zagoda and composed the saucy comic "Tijuana Bibles" on the side. Joseph Bryl, Sr. later worked at National Video on the South Side, a company that made television components. Bryl's mother Mary was a homemaker; during the war she helped manufacture bombs at the National Can Company.

"Where I grew up there was a rigidity as to what was [acceptable] music," said Bryl, who has lived on the South Side all of his sixty-plus years. "We would go to my friend Paul's basement. All the guys would be listening to Derek and the Dominoes, The Allman Brothers' 'Eat a Peach.' I would bring over a Kinks record and a Small Faces album [and they didn't like it.] It didn't have that long jamming they liked. *Creem* magazine would do extensive articles on David Bowie when he was traveling through Asia. I was starting to like Bowie's music and looking at this flamboyant performance artist, trying to balance my liking of his music and the visuals; it took me a moment to transcend my own qualms. None of my friends except for Paul would go with me to punk rock bars in the late 1970s. And that was my first exposure to gay culture in Chicago: seeing a group of [crossdressers] walk into La Mere Vipere."

Shanahan said, "Saving rock was not based in what the Disco Demolition guys were doing when they were running on the field in their worst Black Sabbath T-shirts. We had lost Black Sabbath at that point to some corporate thing at Warner Brothers. They were past *Masters of Reality*. *Deep Purple* had gone the same way. The music changed. As disco got bad, the real heavy, cool rock I was into as a kid had gotten bad, too. Punk rock and house music was the genuine article. And I was drawn to that like a moth to a flame."

The stands at Comiskey Park the day of Disco Demolition

Dennis DeYoung has always had a feisty relationship with rock music critics, many of whom lambasted the lush orchestrations and melodies of Styx. DeYoung was a favorite target of Steve Dahl and Garry Meier, and he was out of the disco realm. But DeYoung's love of the White Sox and his refreshing Chicago-style candor made for one of the more memorable encounters of this book.

Dennis DeYoung was born in 1947 as part of a White Sox family in the far south, working class neighborhood of Roseland. He grew up in a two flat on 101st Place, where Uncle Lee lived on the first floor.

The son of a South Side pressman, DeYoung's code of honor frames his commentary on the White Sox, his friend Tony LaRussa, his not-so-close friend Steve Dahl, and the cultural overtones of Disco Demolition. DeYoung hasn't traveled beyond his family home in the southern suburb of Frankfort.

And here is how South Side loyalty is shaped:

It is 1963, and DeYoung is an avid White Sox fan, particularly fond of Gary Peters, Juan Pizarro, and Pete Ward (they won ninety-four games, only to finish one game behind the New York Yankees). Styx is a year old, formed in the basement of his Roseland home. One afternoon, DeYoung and his friends make a considerable effort to get to Comiskey Park.

"I'd get the bus at 102nd and Michigan in Roseland, go up Michigan, and it hits State Street," he whistled. "No Dan Ryan then." (The last segment of the Ryan expressway opened in 1970.) DeYoung continued, "You get off at 35th Street, you are fine because everyone is there. But to try to beat the crowds, we would go south to 36th, 37th, hide in the bushes, wait for a bus, and go home. We'd run like hell to the factory on 61st Street where my dad worked until he got off work. Then we'd go home with him."

Maury DeYoung was a pressman at American Printing Company at 61st and State. He worked there for forty years. "He carried a metal lunch box," said DeYoung proudly. "It was big and noisy and smelled like giant rolls of fresh paper, some six feet high. His fingernails were permanently blue. People thought it was dirt. It wasn't. It was ink. He would tell me not to end up like him."

Here is how loyalty begins:

The Styx smash "Babe" was released in September 1979, two months after Disco Demolition.

DeYoung wrote the ballad for his wife Suzanne, whom he met in 1964 at a Mendel High School dance in Roseland. The dance was two weeks after DeYoung saw the Beatles on The Ed Sullivan Show.

"I got no axes to grind, I am what I fucking am," he said as a sliver of sunlight cut through his living room. "If it is good polka, I like it. If it is rap and it is fun, I like it. But disco wasn't enough for Steve Dahl. Suddenly rock 'n' roll was in jeopardy because of wimpy ballads. Really? I didn't know [the Beatles'] 'Yesterday' was so wimpy. I was confused. Rock 'n' roll is everything. That's how it got into my shit. I had written a song for my wife's birthday that was never supposed to be a Styx song. I was trying to save money on jewelry, so I thought, 'I'd write her a song.' So I called the Panozzo brothers (Styx's drummer, John, and bassist, Charles) and we did a demo. Bing, bing, done. I sing all the parts. No guitars. It was a gift to my wife. Everybody hears it and said, 'That's a hit record.' I wasn't even trying. I should do that more often."

"Babe" became the lead single from the band's 1979 triple-platinum album *Cornerstone*. It was the first and only American number one single for Styx.

And here is how loyalty sustains:

"Dahl goes from 'It's not only disco killing rock 'n' roll, it's ballads," DeYoung said. "And guess who is his number one culprit? He picks out 'Babe' and blows it up every morning. People called me. I didn't know [Dahl]. They go, 'Dennis, this guy is blowing up your record.' I go, 'What the fuck?' I call my promotion guy and tell him if, he doesn't like the song, that's cool with me. But please, don't blow the thing up. It's a song about my wife and we live in this city. And then for forever I became Dahl's whipping boy. He was relentlessly on me. It was never about me. It was like blowing up records in a fucking baseball stadium. It was about him."

Dahl confirms this. "I blew up that shit," he said.

"Babe" and disco weren't Dahl's only targets. Teenage Radiation guitarist and musical director Roman J. Sawczak grew up in the same Roseland neighborhood as DeYoung. Sawczak's father Walter worked in the steel mills, his mother Anna was a clerk at the famous Gately's People Store in Roseland, owned by Chicago Park District commissioner James T. Gatley.

Sawczak played in a south suburban cover band called Cartune that morphed into Dahl's Teenage Radiation. "So much happened so fast," Sawczak said. "It was the hottest ticket. The best show on radio. I'm in a Top 40 band and the next thing you know I'm at Alpine Valley opening for Foreigner with Teenage Radiation. Our band is a bunch of idiots. Some of the guys on our crew happened to take beer that wasn't for us. So there's a whole thing backstage. Janet [Dahl] was outside the dressing room. The limos from Foreigner pulled up. Security was crazy. I don't know if they pushed Janet out of the way, but Steve flipped out. The next morning one of the first thing Steve does on the radio was play 'Feel Like the First Time.' I'm going, 'Wow, he's playing a Foreigner song after last night, that's crazy.' Then of course about twenty seconds in you hear the needle just scratching across the record back and forth. He goes into the whole story. It was classic radio."

At times, DeYoung cringed when talking about Dahl. He asked, "How did Steve Dahl draw attention to himself? By making fun of Karen Carpenter when she died. 'I'm going to take the high and mighty and bring them low.' I never fought back, but it never stopped. Garry Meier knows me. We're okay ever since he left Dahl. It was Steve and Garry's way of making a living. I get it."

"We're the only rock band from this city who has actually lived here the whole time." (Jim Peterik of the Ides of March and then Survivor also never left Chicago.)

Suzanne DeYoung listened to our conversation while sitting at the white piano where DeYoung composed "Babe." DeYoung nodded towards a crystal trophy on top of the piano. "That's a People's Choice Award; I won that in 1979 for Styx. Not a bad year, 1979. We had four triple platinum albums consecutively. No one had ever done that. [Cornerstone] was the third of the four and a complete departure musically. We toured, which is why I wasn't at Disco Demolition.

"Disco Demolition was sleight of hand. It was 'How do I draw attention to myself?' Is there anything wrong with that in show business? I believe that's applauded. Did Dahl really care about disco? Who cares? Did I care? No. The people that went to see Led Zeppelin in 1978 or Springsteen, or Styx—God bless them—I don't want to put them in the same breath as these giants of musical history. These people never went to a disco? Give me a break. People go to rock concerts because they want to get high and get laid. Why did people go to discos? Same reason. But they wore satin rather than blue jeans."

Styx's musical style evolved in the early 1970s, not in clubs or in emerging discos, but by playing the high school circuit around Chicago. The band learned to be more expressive and did not have to succumb to demands from club owners. The first Styx hit was 1972's "Lady," and fans flooded WLS-AM with phone calls to play the bombastic ballad. But DeYoung said Styx took off in 1975 when A&M Records signed them and released their debut LP *Equinox*. The album sold 1.2 million copies.

Coincidentally, the first hit from *Equinox* was "Lorelei," a name that later would be taken on by WLUP's rock girl.

"A&M never heard one album we made until we gave it to them," DeYoung said. "We produced all the records in Chicago at either Paragon or Pumpkin [studios]. We did what we thought was right, whether that's good, bad, or indifferent. If you hate Styx's music, blame me. If you liked it, give me some credit. The first record we made a lot of money for them, so they said, 'Leave them alone.' But that's how they were. It was an artist's label—Jerry [Moss] and Herb [Alpert]."

When Styx was playing suburban high schools, often times their opening act was M&R Rush, another rock band from the Roseland area. Roman J. Sawczak's first gig in music was in 1975 as a drum tech for M&R Rush. At the time M&R Rush was a cover band that played lots of Uriah Heep. The Loop helped break their original song "Rock and Roll Chicago." Sawczak said, "South Side you think Styx. North Side, I guess you think Billy Corgan, Smashing Pumpkins. Completely different styles of music. South Side is pure rock 'n' roll."

In 1980, Styx was voted the most popular band in America, according to a *Gallup* pool. DeYoung was not concerned about disco cooling the heels of Styx's remarkable run.

"Was I threatened by disco?" asked DeYoung, who left the band in 1999. "No. If you're going to be threatened in 1979, you should be worried about the new wave coming in from England (The Clash, The Jam), not disco. Disco is really about the club and the experience of participating. Disco—people dance. Rock 'n' roll began as dance music, for God's sake. So anyone, Mr. Dahl, Mr. Meier, or whoever claims otherwise, is historically ignorant. I used to watch *American Bandstand*, which was my gateway into a world I didn't know. And what did they do? Dance."

DeYoung got up from his sofa and did a bit of a jig. He says, "Now if you can dance to Styx music, you're a better man than I am. I wasn't trying to make dance music. God forbid, when Rod Stewart did 'Sexy,' I didn't go, 'Oh God no, I think I might have a stroke!' Who gives a shit? It's a fucking piece of music, that's all it is. All that Disco Demolition was about was self-aggrandizing. And as Dahl would tell you, it became so much more than he ever thought it would. I applaud Steve Dahl, for this reason only. It's in 'Gypsy.' "Everybody's gotta have a gimmick. And he had a gimmick."

Garry Meier

7. STEVE AND GARRY

The yin and yang radio personalities attracted a generation of fans. Steve and Garry don't talk to each other these days, but Meier was thoughtful and sometimes wistful in recalling the moments that surrounded Disco Demolition.

Steve Dahl was born in Pasadena, California where he grew up listening to Al Lohman and Roger Barkley, one generation removed from the comedy team of Bob & Ray. The droll sounding Bob Elliott (the late father of actor-writer Chris Elliott) was the foil to the more boisterous Ray Goulding, who died in 1990. Bob & Ray resurrected their career in 1979, spoofing "Do Ya' Think I'm Sexy" on *Saturday Night Live*.

Just like Bob Elliott, Barkley was the straight man, interviewing and channeling Lohman's wide world of characters. Barkley would split from Lohman to become morning personality at KJOI.

Barkley, who died of pancreatic cancer in 1997, never again spoke to Lohman.

"My dad used to listen to them," Dahl recalled in thoughtful tones. "He used to listen to Bob Crane [future star of *Hogan's Heroes*] who was really funny on the radio and Lohman and Barkley. There was a good earthquake in 1971, the Sylmar Earthquake. It was scary because it happened at 6:00 a.m. and you were asleep. I woke up and they were on the clear channel civil defense station. They had a generator that kicked in and they did all these characters, like Ted J. Baloney, who were all huddled in a closet afraid to come out. That was a watershed moment for me in understanding the power of radio. It made me feel okay because they were making jokes about this thing that just happened even though they were still doing the news.

"And the characters were not unlike what I did at WDAI by myself."

On February 23, 1978, Steve Dahl began hosting "Steve Dahl's Rude Awakening" on alternative WDAI in Chicago. Dahl had been pulling a now-impossible 7.2 ratings at WWWW (W4) in Detroit, Michigan. A solo act, Dahl used a dozen imaginary characters that were influenced by the Firesign Theater and the Credibility Gap. His posse included Rex Reational, a gay Tinsel Town reporter, spiritualist Baba Ganoush and an acid-casualty radio producer known as Travis T. Hipp.

On December 24, 1978 Dahl had just completed a live man-on-the-street show three floors below the WDAI studios on Wacker Drive. He was wearing a Santa Claus suit. WDAI general manager Jack Minkow called Dahl to his office. He informed Dahl that, because of low ratings, the station would ditch its rock format and become Chicago's first disco station.

Dahl had only been married four months. His wife Janet left Detroit to live with her husband in southwest suburban Bolingbrook. She quit her job and law school, and her condo had been sold—by her husband on air. There was a lot at stake for the young couple, but Dahl could not picture himself spinning disco records. Dahl was fired. "Technically, I quit," he said. "But it was a constructive firing."

He drove home to Bolingbrook still dressed as Santa Claus. He had unwittingly signed a no-compete contract that prohibited his return to Detroit, so there was no turning back.

"He came home in his Santa outfit," Janet Dahl remembered. "He had a shoebox filled with his stuff. This was before cell phones. He walked in and said, 'I don't have a job. But everything is going to be okay.' Every time Steve lost a job he followed it up with, 'Everything is going to be okay.' At that moment we didn't know how un-okay it was going to be. We thought we'd go to Detroit over the holidays and get hooked up with some station that would be glad to have Steve back. But the no-compete was across all of ABC's stations. We were young. I didn't want to move to California. I was devastated. I had given up my teaching career and law school. Our life was unraveled.

"It was a terrible winter. Steve said to not buy any Christmas presents. So I bought socks and a dartboard and I put a WDAI logo in the middle of it. There was lots of snow and lots of time to sit in the house and grouse and bitch."

Dahl did have a studio in his downstairs bedroom-den. Deploying a four track, a two track, and a mixer, he recorded parody songs and bits reel to reel. "Some of his ideas came from the abundance of idle time he had," Janet said. "When Lee Abrams had The Loop ready to go, some of these songs were already in the

bank, and the notion of rebelling against
WDAI and disco was formed in his head.
My parents didn't say, 'I told you so,' but
they were worried. I know that informed
the rest of Steve's career, because my
Dad would say, 'This is why you have to
have six month's money in the bank.'
You're never safe in radio. I think Steve
has had nine different jobs."

At midnight, 1979 WDAI signed off
as a rock station with Don McLean's
"American Pie," and re-emerged as
a disco station with the Bee Gee's
"Stayin' Alive."

By March 1979 Dahl landed at
WLUP-FM (The Loop). WLUP was
just two years old, having switched over

Steve Dahl with fans

from WSDM (Smack Dab in the Middle). WSDM was owned by the Chess Records family, known for
having only female on-air personalities in the twilight of its run. But when Dahl came to WLUP, he was
quickly paired with all-night jock Garry "Matthew" Meier.

Dahl had found his Roger Barkley.

"When I met Garry, it just seemed very right," Dahl said in a 1989 *Chicago Sun-Times* profile. "I think we
realized right away how much better the two of us were together than by ourselves."

In the fall of 1973, Meier was working construction in Sauk Village, Illinois, when he decided to attend
broadcasting school at the Institute for Broadcast Arts in Chicago. He was spinning Gordon Lightfoot
and Anne Murray at WYEN-FM in Des Plaines during the mid 1970s, and by March 1979, he was WLUP's
all-night jock, playing what would become known as classic rock. Meier listened to Dahl's WLUP "Rude
Awakening" morning show while driving home from his night gig.

"The moment Steve realized he might want to work with me, we were crossing over from my all-night
show to his morning show," Meier recalled. "Because I had listened to him on his show; I knew his sense

of humor. I said, 'Steve Dahl is coming up. He found gasoline in Bolingbrook for 79.9 on the pump, we're going to talk about it.' He heard that and liked the way it sounded. Then he realized there was a syncopation to our senses of humor. We clicked from the get go."

Dave Logan was the WLUP promotion director who decided to pair Dahl and Meier. Over lunch at a near North Side Chicago cafe he explained, "I was getting into work early one day. We had just re-changed the station from The Loop that played Joni Mitchell and Moody Blues records into the 'meat-eating Loop,' which is what we called it. Garry was doing the overnight show, a holdover from the soft Loop. Steve was the new guy, and they started doing crossover at the change of the shift at six in the morning. As the weeks went on, the crossovers became longer and really funny. Steve was in the studio by himself.

"It wasn't how radio is done today with producers, social media people, and squads of people working on a big morning show. I went to the guy who was the program director at the time, Jesse Bullett, and said, 'Have you been listening to Steve in the morning? These guys have a great chemistry happening and I think Steve is comfortable with Garry as a contributor.' Steve needs an audience in the studio because he likes to have face time with the people he's talking with. And Garry was interested in getting off the all-night shift. It instantly started building and building."

Dahl had worked with Lee Abrams at prog rock station WWWW in Detroit, and in 1979 Abrams was a consultant at WLUP. "After my first show Jesse Bullett brought me into his office and started the sound byte after the first thing I said on the air," Dahl recalled. "After sixty seconds he clicks it. I'm still talking. He said, 'After sixty seconds you stop talking. If you can't say it in sixty seconds, don't say it.' I said, 'I gotta go' and I left. Lee Abrams called me at home and said, 'What's going on?' I don't know what he did but I never had to answer to anybody after that."

Abrams and Logan went on to be original staff members of XM satellite radio. "When WDAI went to disco we thought, 'This is great. Steve would fit in right here,'" Logan recalled. "He had the attitude and the kind of swagger that was serving the tone of the radio station at the time. Steve is a smart ass. Garry was the sophisticate.

"Garry could be as guttural as anybody and certainly had a wickedly sarcastic streak. We used to have a daily paper called *The Looper* and he wrote it like he was writing for the *Onion*. Steve was a smart-aleck guy who would say things everybody was thinking, but when he said, 'disco sucks,' he meant it. He actually had a well-evaluated reason why he did, because it was a bunch of blue-collar people who were getting this disco lifestyle shoved down their throat by the media. It wasn't because WDAI had gone disco. That was a blip passing on the expressway. It was that a lot of America was fed up with this superficiality. It permeated everything at the time, looking a certain way, acting a certain way, portraying an affluence whether it was true or not, because you were 'disco.'"

Dahl recalled, "When I started on The Loop I started making fun of 'DAI and disco music. They said I could stay [at WDAI] but I would have played three twenty-minute records every hour. I was making fun of it before I hooked up with Garry. We'd play a record and I'd scratch the needle across the record and blow it up."

Every day.

Dahl encouraged his Loop fans to show up at WDAI appearances and throw marshmallows at the station's van. "It was *yes* to Old Style and T-shirts, and *no* to choreography and three-piece suits," he said. "It was fun, stupid, and spontaneous." When the acclaimed producer-songwriter Van McCoy died suddenly of a massive heart attack on July 6, 1979, Dahl destroyed McCoy's biggest hit "The Hustle" on the air. McCoy was thirty-nine years old. McCoy was a major musical force, writing the Barbara Lewis R&B hit "Baby I'm Yours" and "I Get the Sweetest Feeling" for Jackie Wilson.

Meier began doing morning news for Dahl and the team took off. Dahl told Meier to drop the "Matthew" shtick and go with his real name Garry. "Steve and Garry" clicked with similar sparks of vintage Albert Brooks (whom they each cited as an influence), working from three basic emotions: despair, excess, and insecurity. Like Brooks and the late Andy Kaufman, Dahl and Meier used those characteristics to break down barriers between imagination and perception, forcing the audience to react.

Disco Demolition was held just four months after Dahl and Meier became a team; their energy was fresh. "The real sweet spot of our career was yet to come," Meier said. "The best work we did, for me, was three or four years later where we got to a rhythm of what the duo was. Our career went fifteen years after that. But Disco Demolition definitely jump started us. Steve had been out of 'DAI for about three months, so we started talking about what happened at WDAI. It was very organic. He took a disco record off the turntable and broke it over his head on the air. You could hear the record breaking. It kept building. And obviously our listenership tapped into it right away. They had been feeling the same thing. We started doing nightclubs. We did Mother's, Pointe East in Lynwood. We did Flipside Records. The crowds were pretty massive for nightclubs, thousands of people.

"At the same time, Skylab was getting ready to fall back to earth. So at these appearances we would wear hardhats with bacon wrapped around them because we knew if Skylab was coming it was coming by the bacon starting to sizzle. People always ask, 'Were you guys high on the air?' No, we weren't. You couldn't write stuff like this. You couldn't ask for a better vortex of things coming together. It was tailor made for our senses of humor and people fed off it. Let's be honest, at that point, Wally Phillips had dominated radio in this town for at least fifteen years before we got going. WGN was your parents' and grandparents' station. We were doing an 'us against them' mentality, 'us against your parents radio.' That isn't the case now. This is just commerce."

Dahl smiled. "During Skylab, Garry was living in an imaginary Winnebago and buried it underground. We were hiding there, kind of an homage to Lohman and Barkley. [Teenage Radiation] did 'Skylab' to (the Rolling Stones 1978 hit) 'Shattered.' There were a lot of things happening, hostages, the Ayatollah, disco. It was a good time just to be a smart ass kid. We were at the same age of the audience becoming more socially aware. And everybody was on the same page, it was not divided like it is now. If you were young, you were pretty liberal."

Meier pointed out, "In fact, less than two years after Disco Demolition we weren't even on that station. We still had the audience but the corporate mentality was afraid of everything: violating community standards. We got caught in the FCC witch hunt blade. There was an atmosphere of dialing down freedom of speech."

Disco Demolition received international attention, and Dahl and Meier were all over the map. "We'd go around the country doing remotes and we'd turn on local radio and there was a Steve and Garry clone in every city," Meier continued. "It was the launch pad. Everything that came after was kind of wrapped around that moment. But we had to deliver. We couldn't live off that for the next fourteen years, and we didn't."

Dahl and Meier attracted fans like future *Chicago Tribune* sportswriter Paul Sullivan, who attended Disco Demolition at the age of nineteen. "Steve was so different than anything that was on Chicago radio at the time," Sullivan said. "He spoke to our generation. He was funny. That was before 'politically correct' was even a term. They were doing something we had never heard before—the comedy and social commentary."

In 1981, Sullivan was hired by the *Tribune* as a copy clerk, and between 1984 and 1987 he was leg man for the late Pulitzer Prize columnist Mike Royko, a long suffering Cubs fan.

"Steve was on the air poking fun at Royko," Sullivan recalled. "I mentioned it to him. He respected Steve. But anyone that attacked him, Royko was guns out and he would blast them. I said, 'Why don't you blast Steve Dahl?' He answered, 'The eagle does not hunt the fly.' I guess he thought Steve was irrelevant, which to him, he probably was. But not to my generation."

Chicago rock radio legend Bob Sirott snagged his first on air gig at WBBM-FM the summer of 1971. He was twenty-three years old in 1973 when he moved to WLS-AM and gained notoriety in the afternoon drive time slot. He saw how Dahl and Meier were branding beyond the borders of traditional radio. "I went into television in 1980 and Dahl was a perfect example of what was going on," Sirott explained one afternoon after his WGN-AM show he hosts with his wife Marianne Murciano. "I saw the younger guys coming into radio and they were different than we were. [Jonathan] Brandmeier, Dahl, Kevin Matthews, and those Loop guys were extremely talented in many different areas. We [at WLS] were trying

Bob Sirott

to push the limit by getting an extra thirty seconds between records. These guys were doing more talk radio; a lot more than we were doing. It's almost like what you saw with Letterman, looking around and seeing the landscape with social media and viral videos and realizing that's just not who he is. He could do it, but he didn't want to. It was time to move on."

Meier had trouble analyzing the chemistry he had with Dahl.

"If I could bottle that I'd be a billionaire," Meier said. "You can't force a Penn and Teller, Trey Parker and Matt Stone, or a Key and Peele. I like watching other duos. I like to think of how they got together, how their chemistry works and how it sustains.

"After we broke up, I talked to Siskel and Ebert and Penn and Teller about their relationships. I wanted to see what kept them on track. It is mutual respect for the duo. One isn't bigger than the other, you just respect the partnership. The one that really hit me was Abbott and Costello. I read their last contract together—Bud got forty percent and Lou got sixty percent. That fucked up Bud Abbott's head. He was never the same. The duo broke apart shortly thereafter and Lou died shortly thereafter. When you are creating something, it is fifty-fifty or nothing. If not, it will blow up at some time. Look at Martin and Lewis. Just keep it to yourself if you think you are the star. It is working for a reason. That's how it went for us for almost fifteen years.

"And then it didn't."

The split was brewing, but on September 13, 1993, Meier quit while on honeymoon with Cynthia Fircak, offended by on air remarks made by Dahl.

Roman J. Sawczak was guitarist in Dahl's Teenage Radiation, and during the mid-1980s he produced the Steve and Garry show for WLUP. "There's been no one better as a duo," he said. "When they split, I understood. For Garry, it wasn't as much as 'I'm pissed.' He needed something different. You gotta remember, Steve is sober now. A lot of times I think, 'If he had sobered up sooner, would I have stuck around? Would Garry have stuck around longer? It was pretty rough at times. I would house sit for Steve when he was gone. One night when Janet was gone, we went to see Dwight Twilley at Park West. We got home to Steve's house, and I think we stayed up until eight in the morning being reckless. He told the station he couldn't come in that afternoon. So he called in and did the show laying on his couch. Garry was pissed, 'Really? You partied all night and you're not going to come into work?'"

In 1996, Rick Kogan of the *Chicago Tribune* wrote that Dahl took two-thirds of the duo's salary, estimated to be in the neighborhood of $6.5 million, for the last five years of their contract, paying Meier himself. In 1989 (when Dahl and Meier were on their second go-round at WLUP) the *Chicago Sun-Times* reported that Dahl made $850,000 a year, from which he paid Meier.

Dahl and Meier split in September 1993, but they had periodic one-off reunions. Once at Chicago's Oak Street Beach in 2006, and on the twenty-eighth anniversary of Disco Demolition, in 2007, when Meier joined Dahl on his WCKG morning show.

 When asked if he would work with Meier again, Dahl said he wouldn't be opposed. "The ball is in their court and I'm not sure of their point of view," Dahl said. "I wouldn't mind it if he came here [to WLS-AM], did his own show, and we'd talk once in a while."

Logan spoke on the subject: "Their best work lasted for decades. I was there for their falling out, too. I was program director at The Loop when they broke up—right after we had been in Dallas at the R&R (Radio & Records) convention trying to sell our super station idea. We had the Mount Rushmore of rock: Steve and Garry in the mornings, Kevin [Matthews] in the mid-days, Brandmeier in the afternoons, Bonaduce at night. Before the convention, Steve wanted to call Garry on his honeymoon. I'm in my office and I'm going,

'I'm glad Garry is in Italy.' Well, somebody had been recording all the stuff. Garry had expressed to me when I came back to The Loop, he didn't know how much longer he and Steve were going to be together.

"They are really one of the quintessential broadcast teams from the 1980s and '90s." (In the early 2000s, Dahl was on WCKG-FM, and Meier was paired with Roe Conn on WLS-FM.)

In September 2015, Dahl was sitting in his ninth floor State Street office after his drive-time shift, ironically on WLS-AM. A large black and white portrait of Steve and Garry doing a remote at the old Great America amusement park hung in a hallway outside his office door.

As time passes, humor evolves.

"To experiment with anything now it has to be right down the center," Dahl continued. "You can see how people now get their careers destroyed in one sentence," Dahl continued. "There's not even any discourse. You're wrong if you don't ascribe to exactly the way I think. I say more on the podcast, but on the radio I don't talk about politics."

Actor-comedian Richard Lewis disagreed with the accusations that Disco Demolition was a homophobic event. "You can't go back in time. You can't go back now and say Disco Demolition was homophobic. It's absurd. Why was it homophobic? Because Donna Summer had a gay following? That never crossed my mind. Disco Demolition was just a comment that this music sucks. It had nothing to do with sexual preference. Disco Demolition couldn't have been staged any better. If the same thing had been done at Carnegie Hall, they would have gotten a standing ovation for the sheer balls of it all."

Logan carefully reflected, "We live in a world today where everybody has an opinion and everybody has a place to put it. Post it. Take pictures of it. Nobody came in [Comiskey Park] to try and prove anything. It was a celebration of rock 'n' roll being something to believe in. And disco represented the bad guy; 1979 was a cusp period in rock 'n' roll, with bands like The Clash and the Jam—English angry bands. Chicago has always been a good hard rocking town. We were trying to stand up for rock, but in all transparency, also saying disco sucks. We were not that altruistic."

Steve Dahl's career has been shaped by uncanny candor and truth. His memorable podcasts of October 2014, detailed the final weeks of the life of his father Roger, who was battling terminal cancer. Dahl had become estranged from his father, and his podcast revealed their reconciliation process.

His wife Janet is a regular weekly character on his WLS-AM show and his podcast. They discuss real life issues with the rhythm of the long-married couple they are. The front door to their house is open. There is no bouncer.

"Some parts of it have been really hard," Janet Dahl said. "When I was a teacher and we were living together, I couldn't let him talk about that [on air]. He'd still talk about 'Miss J the Teacher' he was living with. I told him that had to stop. He announced my pregnancy with Pat. My parents heard that because he was on the air in Detroit. I've never pushed back that much because that is part of the way we have grown. He is very somber at home and doesn't work too hard to make me laugh. He had a few characters he would use when he was really in trouble, like 'Mr. Garden Hose,' that would tickle me. That was out of character because he's not that person."

Janet agrees to appear on the show with her husband because her balance humanizes his radio personality. "He has sort of a didactic drive to make it his show," she explained. "Sometimes he wants someone else to say he's not really a hard ass and he's okay, and that would be me. Even though we fight and sometimes fight on the radio. But it lets people see him as I see him."

"I always felt honesty is what you should be doing in radio," Steve said. "Part of it is that it's easier to not have to remember made up shit. And the sheer volume of content you have to pump out, you have to rely on the truth. Besides Lohman and Barkley, the other thing I listened to as a kid in LA was KPPC, which was an underground station where everybody was honest. My first job in radio was there. They used to say everything that was happening. That format didn't last. Then all FM stations became super formatted and nobody talked. I went to Detroit to work at WABX, which was their freeform station. They changed formats to lite rock on my way there. Everybody hated it, but because it was such a vacuum, it was a chance for me to talk and try different things."

Honesty resonated with the rock audiences of the Disco Demolition generation, framed against disco's glitter and concern with status. "Nobody on radio was [being honest]," Dahl said. "It was, 'Here's this guy and he's saying the things I think, too.' It was hard to do because nobody wanted me to talk. I think I'm pretty funny now, but I'm not sure how funny I was then.

Lorelei Shark throws the first pitch while Steve Dahl looks on

Steve Dahl on the field during Disco Demolition

8. CHICAGO RADIO OF THE LATE 1970S

Freeform FM radio began in the late 1960s. Terri Hemmert was the mysterious all-night jock during the mid-1970s at progressive WXRT-FM in Chicago. Out on the left coast, Los Angeles freeform jock Jim Ladd became a metaphor for Tom Petty's 2002 album The Last DJ, *about dwindling freedom of musical expression. Ladd was let go from KLOS radio in 2011 when Cumulus Broadcasting took over Citadel Broadcasting. Ladd's fans were called "The Tribe," not unlike Dahl and Meier's "Insane Coho Lips." Just as Dahl found freedom in podcasts, Ladd is now heard on satellite radio. Freeform radio opened the doors for Disco Demolition.*

WDAI-FM (94.7) radio launched in 1971 as a progressive rock station, poised to take on WXRT-FM next door at 93.1. WDAI got off to an inauspicious start when ABC messed up the call letters. WDAI actually stood for Detroit Auto Industry and the Chicago station was supposed to be WRIF. The station moved to album rock until late 1978.

By mid-1979, WDAI was cultivating a hip urban audience, becoming the first Chicago station to play mixes. Future Hot Mix 5 member Kenny Jason played mixes on WDAI along with pioneers like Lou DeVito and Scott Adams.

"Everyone got so mad when WDAI went from rock to disco." Joe Shanahan recalled. "But I didn't want to hear the Eagles. I didn't like Journey. The music was vapid. We were urban kids. I wasn't into that fake cowboy bullshit. We were attracted to punk rock. House. Or that urban disco sound that was like rhythm.

"Rod Stewart doing disco just wasn't right. Bette Midler? It might have been accepted because she came out of the bath house scene. I kind of got Cher doing it, it was weird and funny. I mean, KISS did a disco song! Casablanca was the big disco label and Donna Summer was great. [Summer's producer-songwriter Giorgio] Moroder—that was the beat. So when we would go to the Warehouse or the Playground, we would hear the stripped down versions, the dub side, the instrumental side. Frankie [Knuckles] and Ron Hardy, all the DJs we were following were doing that. I remember going to the Bistro and hearing Lou DeVito play some strange B-side of 'Love to Love You Baby.' One night I was at the Bistro and Jimmy Page and Robert Plant were there. It was this blend of what rock is and what culture is."

Dahl hit on the oddball blend of rock and American Gothic Midwestern radio. He was driving around Chicago with his wife Janet in their Renault when they heard beloved WGN-AM morning man Wally Phillips on the car radio. The grandfatherly Phillips liked to say he started every show with a big smile on his face. He believed a voice sounds different when you smile, and the listener can sense that.

"I had never heard him before," Dahl recalled. "I never made fun of him at WDAI. When I heard him I thought, 'This is the worst thing ever.' As soon as I got back on the radio [at WLUP], I started making fun of him and WDAI because they fired me.

"And remember, disco was pretty mainstream. An ABC-owned station would not have switched to an all disco format if they didn't think it was a popular thing. Wally Phillips got mad and started talking about me . . . Kids were listening, too. They had no one else to listen to. So that was happening while I was making fun of disco. It was this bizarre convergence of these two things. It wasn't like some master plan."

Chicago radio and television personality Bob Sirott does not have pleasant memories of the pop music landscape of the 1970s. In July 1979, he was the popular drive time afternoon jock on WLS-AM, "The Big 89."

"The seventies were the worst decade for music ever," Sirott declared. "The only good part of the decade was you had the singer-songwriters like Carole King and James Taylor in the early part of the seventies. But then you had the DeFranco Family, Bay City Rollers, The Osmonds, Terry Jacks. Throw in some bad disco, even though they were actually better produced records aside from the singer-songwriters." He paused and added, "There was [1979's] 'My Sharona' by the Knack."

Former Styx composer-keyboardist Dennis DeYoung said, "Rock music is an economic force, period. End of story. If a radio station could get away with playing the same song all day long and have the highest ratings in Chicago, what would happen? They would play the same song all day long. That's why I sing for my supper. Don't call me an 'artist.' I don't buy that shit. The first thing all musicians do is sign a record deal that tells us just how much we're going to make per record. That's a commercial artist at the very least.

"When Jon Landau finally figured out [he should] take the fucking newsboy cap and beard off of Bruce Springsteen and be James Dean, that was a calculated marketing ploy. How about Elvis-fucking-Costello? I bet you've read a lot of good stuff about Elvis in your lifetime. Good for you. Guess what he did? He fucking faked you out. He put on those glasses, stood like a geek, and jumped around the stage to get noticed so he could make all these other fucking records. But there you are, 'He's an artist, oh God!' Once in a while you get a guy like Kurt Cobain, who had terrible emotional problems. And he was what he appeared to be. But the vast majority of us are trying to be Elvis. So I sing for my supper."

Dahl and Meier changed the game in Chicago by being themselves.

A generation of AM rock listeners grew up listening to the WLS charms of Clark Weber, the cynicism of Larry Lujack, and understated wit of Bob Sirott. When it got wild at night, there was John Landecker's "Boogie Check," WCFL's Barney Pip (who told listeners to "turn into peanut butter") and the "Subterranean Circus" of Ron Britain. The newfound freedom of FM radio enabled Dahl and Meier to play less music and lampoon current events. Dahl was a forerunner in the field. "Before I caught on at WWWW [in Detroit] people were instructed to just play records and not talk," he said. "At WABX [also in Detroit] they told me not to give the time on a morning show because it 'bummed people out.'"

Richard Lewis has been a frequent guest on Dahl's radio shows. "I've known Steve and Howard [Stern] since the early 1980s," Lewis said in a phone interview. "It was the most fun I've ever had on radio. They were pioneers. It's like looking at a rock chart and seeing The Byrds. David Crosby goes down and hangs out with Stephen Stills. And then Neil Young comes in. Steve and Howard are on top of one of the most important trees in the history of radio. They had courage and conviction. It started a whole new wave of mostly inferior 'shock jocks.'"

Born in Brooklyn in 1947, Lewis was influenced by Lenny Bruce, Richard Pryor, and the reality-bending characters of Jonathan Winters—voices who were not unlike Dahl's radio-theater characters of the late 1970s. "There were way fewer comedians in 1979," he said. "In the late seventies and early eighties, if you were going to be edgy there was the Bill Hicks-Sam Kinison type of comedians who I loved and that [weren't] politically correct at all. People either got praise for it or lost their career. Through all of that I've worshipped Steve Dahl."

Rick Wojcik, owner of Dusty Groove, was born in 1966 in the South Side neighborhood of Beverly, but by the time he was ten, his family moved to the southern suburb of Frankfort, where they lived in DeYoung's neighborhood.

"In 1974, 75 WLS was the major station," Wojcik said. "You heard early disco, novelty songs, glam, and glitter rock. It was all mixed together. You would have [C.W. McCall's 1975 country hit] 'Convoy' next to [Carol Douglas's 1974 disco hit] 'Doctor's Orders.' You would go to the beach in the summer and every radio was on WLS. It became the same thing with The Loop, where their (black) rock T-shirts were everywhere. I remember being at Chicago Fest and wondering, 'Where do I get this free T-shirt?' There was an unconscious multicultural environment to WLS, and to WCFL, to a lesser extent. I also grew up on K-TEL compilations, Kool and the Gang next to Elton John. Then the rise of The Loop and WMET pre-dated [Disco Demolition]. I was young at the time but I could feel it. There clearly was this dividing line you saw at Chicago Fest, things like that. But Disco Demolition certainly crystalized that moment.

"I see it now when I look at record collections. People who started buying in 1977, '79. It got very segmented. Where if you look at someone who was buying mainstream stuff in late 1960 and early '70s, they easily had a fair amount of black and white. I would also throw in gay and straight. Glam? David Bowie?"

Wojcik listened to Dahl and Meier in 1979. "Steve was very funny," said Wojcik, who opened his first Dusty Groove in 1996 in the Hyde Park neighborhood, south of Comiskey Park. "I'm slowly going back to him now [on WLS-AM]. He's completely honest about all his insecurities. There was a mixed message that got taken the wrong way. He had a good sense of self. He did 'Do Ya' Think I'm Disco', and a lot of people went, 'Those guys hate gays,' I think it's the same thing as people listening to Randy Newman's 'Short People,' and saying, 'He hates little people.' It's like having a rally with a leader talking about peace and then rioting breaks out because they are so inspired by his message. Obviously, this was not about peace."

Dahl was dressed as a general storming the field. War was declared.

By 1980, disco was defeated on mainstream Chicago radio and WDAI switched to the Top 40/oldies mixed format it has today as WLS-FM. On February 6, 1981, Dahl was fired by WLUP for "continued assaults on community standards." Meier was offered Dahl's gig, but refused it in a show of solidarity. On February 23, 1981, the team signed a five-year contract with WLS-FM, which of course, used to be WDAI.

"The other album rock station in town was WMET," Dahl recalled. "I get fired and Garry comes along with me. We meet at the Hyatt with [WMET General Manager] Bruce Holberg and he doesn't believe we got fired. He thinks we're fucking pranking him. I'm like, 'Dude, this is real, you'll reap all these rewards.' He didn't believe it. I ended up having to buy lunch, four corned beef sandwiches that were four bucks each. It was weird, like, 'What do I have to do to prove to you I got fired?' So then John Gehron [program director of WLS] called." Steve and Garry were resurrected on the afternoon drive shift on WLS-FM.

Dave Logan was the WLUP promotion director behind Disco Demolition. "The echo after that, WLUP went through the roof," Logan explained. "It became the first FM radio station to beat WLS-AM. The station was 3.1 when we started the format change. After Disco Demolition we were 7.4. We were beating WLS in double digits. A lot of that was perception as opposed to the way they do it today with electronic measurement."

Michaels laughed and said, "If you look at the history of WDAI, even I get confused. For about ten years they had six or seven formats. They did a thing called Kicks Country there for a couple years."

In 1991 the late Randy Michaels (Clear Channel Communication, *Chicago Tribune*) even took a quick swing with dance and rap tunes accented by Gulf War updates in Spanish on what was called "HELL 94.7."

Radio of the late 1970s reflected the community, and listeners felt ownership towards their stations and their music. In the early 1970s, Andy Frain ushers were hired to manage the crowds of teenagers who would watch radio personalities like Larry Lujack, Bob Sirott, Clark Weber and John Landecker work from behind a glass window.

Jim Peterik explained, "Chicago radio was more home grown, more folksy. L.A. had its scene, it was very slick. We had guys like Art Roberts, Dick Biondi, Dex Card, Jim Stagg. They all felt like your friends. We [Ides of March] thought we were done with [our 1970 hit] 'Vehicle,' and the band and our managers went to see Art Roberts [at WLS-AM]. He was the kingmaker. He listens to it and says, 'You've got a number one record if you put in call and response: 'Love you/love you, Need you/need you.' We go, 'You're right.' We missed that. We trusted him. They would talk about the songs. A lot of cities were formatted song, song, song, a little bit of talk. Our stations were personality jocks. In the late 1960s and early 1970s, WCFL and WLS had a local playlist. That was significant. Without that we couldn't have broken out of Chicago. Given you had a good record, the station played it. That became a springboard for 'Vehicle,' [The Bucking-hams'] 'Kind of a Drag' and all these songs."

Sirott explained, "Radio has been more important to people in Chicago. I know personalities in New York and Los Angeles who are very good and very creative. People don't care about them as much as they care here. New York has Broadway, Los Angeles has Hollywood and the movies. We don't have any of that. Plus, we have a climate that is conducive to activities that are not outside. You are in the car with your radio. You are at home with your radio. Andy Frain ushers controlling the crowd? It is crazy when you think of it now. I remember in the 1970s, I had an appearance to make at a Champaign [Illinois] drive-in. About 8:30 at night I stopped at some fast food joint, and I heard [John] Landecker on the radio [from Chicago]. It dawned on me, you get out of Chicago a bit and there is nothing to do. FM wasn't happening yet. There's more happening outside of New York and Los Angeles. You get outside of Chicago and there's just corn.

"When I got to WLS-AM in 1973, I worked at night for a couple months before they moved me to the afternoon. You have the powerful stations in L.A. spilling most of their wattage into the Pacific Ocean. The Atlantic [Ocean] in New York. Here, we are in the middle of the country.

"It is a blow torch going everywhere."

Dahl recalled, "In Chicago at that time there was WXRT, which was still an underground station. The Loop was the album station. WMET. There were a maximum of two FM album stations and Top 40. I don't even think there was lite rock or any of that yet. We used to get six, seven, eight shares then. Nobody does that now."

Logan explained, "We were coming out of the singer-songwriter era, the Eagles, Joni Mitchell. The new Loop was, 'Good morning, it's 9 a.m., here's AC/DC!' the Loop wore its rock persona loud and proud. We had a lot of attitude. The logo, which is still around almost forty years later, is iconic."

Chicago artist and writer Tony Fitzpatrick pointed out, "Whenever you saw busts for ten pounds of PCP, they would drag out six assholes wearing Loop T-shirts."

Former WLUP general sales manager Jeff Schwartz had been hired away from WMET where he was an account executive. Schwartz explained, "WMET was a lighter version of The Loop. The Loop did personalities better than anybody else. What made WXRT was that they didn't play commercials, they read commercials. Everybody can play the same music, but it was the delivery in radio back then. Obviously Dahl and Meier were so over the top unique, but don't forget, Mitch Michaels' 'Yeah, Baby' was so integral to the sound. The Loop had the greatest night time jock in the history of rock 'n' roll: Sky Daniels. Anybody can play Rush or the Beatles. But nobody could intro and outro the music and the image of the station more than the on air talent of The Loop."

Meier said, "Disco Demolition was the last moment where radio had the power to get everybody together. Or even broadcast television. What event has happened since? I imagine in the nineties Howard Stern got his fan base together when he needed them to get together. Thousands of people showed up for his events, but it wasn't Disco Demolition. It is sad to watch the erosion of that conduit to the fan. If you get a fraction of the audience we had you are considered successful today, because the bar has been lowered so much. Corporations have just squeezed the life out of radio stations. Is there a destination show in Chicago everyone is talking about right now? It's all fragmented."

Logan argued, "It was a notable and undeniable sense of community, but to say it hasn't happened in radio since is oversimplifying it. There's different kinds of community: the whole NPR community, that's a world built on community as an identity. Country stations and Top 40 stations all have their summer jams. [But] I will say there was a fierce identification with what we captured there."

Dahl does not think Disco Demolition would happen in 2016.

"And now seeing it reframed the way people reframed it, people would say it is racist and homophobic," he said. "People do look at everything differently now. It always seems unfair to me to judge the event on modern day criteria. But I don't verbalize that very well. We were funny and all that shit, but Garry and I played six to eight records an hour. That was an important part of what the Loop was. Our thinking wasn't that sophisticated."

Meier agreed. "I never saw homophobia or racism remotely connected," he said. "The Bee Gees were a main focus because of the movie [*Saturday Night Fever*]. They're white. In all the interactions we had with the fans, there never was any racist or homophobic rhetoric. Never.

"People today are looking at Disco Demolition through their lens. They are equating hip-hop and rap with disco. There are similarities, but you are looking at it in a politically correct society, more so now than back then. It is very sensitive today. You are not going to get away with stuff you did thirty-five, forty years ago. Could you put All In the Family on [network] television today? The answer is mostly no. The game is so tight, everybody is afraid to blow off their foot and regroup. Companies aren't going to support you as much. It is a whole different mindset."

Schwartz said, "It is nothing more than Steve losing his job at WDAI when they changed to disco. Disco, for all rock 'n' rollers, was very easy to hate. Steve blew up disco records on the air because of disco and what happened at 'DAI. Simple. Period. End of story."

Dahl, Meier, Veeck, and Schwartz do not keep in touch. But Veeck agreed Disco Demolition was never intended to have any discriminatory overtones.

"Never," Veeck declared. "That is revisionist history. It is ludicrous. "

Just two days after graduating college, Veeck became guitarist-drummer in Chattanooga Glass, a rock-soul band that played the Delaware–Virginia club circuit. "It was great," he reflected. "Chattanooga Glass manufactured liquor bottles. We were a good cover band. When I heard this disco thing I was sitting in a bar on Route 13. We were on break. Sunday was the only day we were allowed to drink on stage. People would come back from the ocean and we'd start at two in the afternoon. KC and the Sunshine Band comes on during the break. Four hundred people who had just been loving us with 'Mustang Sally' and 'Brown Sugar' got up and danced to KC and the Sunshine Band. I said to my bass player, 'Mike, this is not good. Not only is this a terrible song, but look at these people.' That's what was in the air.

"Of course I'm sorry that Disco Demolition happened in some ways. But I would never want someone to think it was homophobic or racist. Given our track records—and I say that for Steve Dahl, too—that is preposterous. I believe that all started with the Gibb brothers, even if Dave Marsh wrote about it the next day."

Mitch Michaels said, "I didn't feel it was racist and homophobic. Being around Steve [Dahl] for a year and a half, he was a pain in the ass, no question about that. A very self-involved guy, self-promoting, but he was absolutely brilliant. Racist and homophobic never entered into my head. I've tried to preach to my kids racist circumstances perpetuate racism. My oldest son happens to be gay. It is wrong to judge any-body. There was no subject off-limits to Steve. He would do and say anything. Trust me. I woke up enough mornings when I was his boss [as WLUP program director from December 1979 through August 1980] and he was reading my memos on the air, calling me a little bitch."

South Side native and Disco Demolition vendor Bob Chicoine reflected, "Much like rock 'n' roll, white [people] had taken over disco by that point. I used to go to discos. There was one a half block from where I lived and Harry [Caray] always mispronounced it: Xanadu [on Broadway at Devon in Rogers Park]. Har-ry would try to pronounce the x, like 'ex-anadu.' It was a cool scene."

Steve Dahl

Steve Dahl entering The Original Mother's

9. DISCO

Disco is not a four-letter word . . .

Disco blossomed from funk, soul, electronics, and measured micro-beats. The smash 1977 film *Saturday Night Fever* crossed the eclectic nocturnal sound into a mainstream landscape where it could be easily satirized. Dahl seized the moment.

He was spot on.

Consider this: The Villlage People's 1978 smash disco hit "Y.M.C.A." remains a standard at many of baseball's major and minor league stadiums, including Wrigley Field. The Village People were created by French producer and former hairdresser Jacques Morali. In the 2010 Alice Echols book *Hot Stuff: Disco and the Remaking of American Culture* Village People "Leatherman" Glenn Hughes believed Morali, who was gay, was intrigued with gays taking on strong, positive, American stereotypes like the cowboy, Native American, cop, and sailor.

Disco's global reach is rarely discussed, but it was powerful and has more artistic staying power than many of the novelty hits (like Village People, Lipps, Inc., Carl Douglas's "Kung Fu Fighting") that cracked America's Top 40 charts.

Between 1978 and 1985, the soundtracks for Pakistani films in Lollywood were shaped by the magnificent disco, electro pop, and seminal house music of Ann Data. "Disco Dildar ('Party Time')" resurfaced in 2015 as part of the Sounds of Wonder! series on Finders Keepers Records. Would Reggaeton have happened without rapid fire, salsa-disco beats?

On another level, The Original Mother's, known colloquially as just "Mother's," is the longest running dance club in America. In 1999, Paul Rosenfeld, founder of CASEO, the Chicago Area Social & Entertainment Organization, told the *Chicago Sun-Times*, "It's the longest running dance club in Chicago under single ownership that I'm aware of. As far as the rest of the country, I can't say."

Tom Gorsuch opened Mother's in 1968 in a former 1940s-era cafeteria. Gorsuch bought the space for $25,000 when it was a dance music club called the Spirit of '76. He re-named the club The Original Mother's after the cocktail lounge featured in the 1960s detective television series *Peter Gunn*. Scenes from the 1986 Rob Lowe and Demi Moore film *About Last Night* were shot in the 8,500 square foot club, framed by red wooden walls.

Dahl made a promotional appearance at Mother's a few months before Disco Demolition. He arrived in a Jeep wearing his general's uniform. Dahl wore a large, handmade cardboard razor blade as a nod to the popularity of cocaine. He also carried a soup ladle spray painted gold to represent a cocaine spoon. Mother's held about 600 people for a concert, and the place was packed.

Gorsuch ran the club from 1968 until 1981. "In the late 1970s it became kind of a discotheque," he said without a smile. "We shut down for three months in 1981 and remodeled. No question disco hurt us. Bands faded out. Chaka Khan was our house band [with Ask Rufus]. Wayne Cochran [and the C.C. Riders]

TOP TEN SELLING DISCO RECORDS (IN NO PARTICULAR ORDER) AT DUSTY GROOVE, FALL 2015

"The perceptions of disco are always evolving," said store owner Rick Wojcik. "So the big hits of mainstream disco years have really been shaken off as folks dig so much deeper, [globally] as well. All compilations show there's a very strong interest in disco from the late 1970s that goes way past clichés and hits. The scene was far deeper than any Disco Demolition crowd would have known."

1. "Bombay Disco" (Various artists) Disco Hits from Hindi Films 1979 to 1985 (Cultures of Soul)
2. "Philadelphia Roots" Funk Soul & the Roots of Disco 1965 - 73 (Soul Jazz, UK)
3. "British Hustle" (Various) "The Sound of British Funk & Disco 1974 to 1982 (Soul Jazz, UK)
4. "Disco Dildar" DIY Disco From the Pakistani Pop Workshop (Finders Keepers, UK)
5. "Disco Italia" Essential Italian Disco 1977 to 1985 (Strut, UK)
6. "Overdose of the Holy Ghost" (Various), The Sound of Gospel Through the Disco & Boogie Eras (Z Records, UK)
7. "Real Sound of Chicago & Beyond" (Various), Underground Disco and Boogie (BBE, UK)
8. "Lagos Disco Inferno" 1975 to 1981, 12 Red Hot Slices From The Golden Era of Nigerian Disco (Academy)
9. "Hustle - Reggae Disco: Kingston London New York" (Various), (Soul Jazz UK)
10. "Disco Love" (Various) Rare Disco and Soul Uncovered (2 CDS), (BBE, UK).

played here on a Sunday night when we just got our lease. Styx played here. Hugh Hefner came here with [painter] LeRoy Neiman. But after we reopened we went to disco. We never had a DJ before that. We put in tables and chairs, we livened it up. We were packed.

"Everybody likes a good dancer."

Detroit Tigers pitcher and organ player Denny McLain visited Mother's at the dawn of disco. McLain was married to Hall of Famer Lou Boudreau's daughter and the Boudreau family lived in the south suburb of Dolton. Future disco singer Rod Stewart visited Mother's decked out in a yellow suit, according to Gorsuch.

Mother's has always had a 4 a.m. liquor license. Mother's always had disco-era pick up lines like: "Are those pants sprayed with Windex? Because I can see myself in them."

Veteran Chicago club disc jockey and cultural historian Joe Bryl said, "During the Disco Demolition period I would go to Mother's to see fledgling punk bands. I saw the B-52s there. Those were pre-Wax Trax! [the Lincoln park record store] shows. [In 1979 and '80] Wax Trax! would book the Buzzcocks and Magazine to play Mother's. Maybe one hundred people came to see a Cramps show there. You would go there, and there were rock 'n' roll guys from 87th and Cicero that thought we were a bunch of faggots because we were listening to this peculiar music. Later it was interesting how bands like Talking Heads and P.I.L. incorporated disco sounds."

Chris Ryan is Vice President of the Lodge Management Group, the umbrella company for Division Street area bars like Mother's, the Lodge Tavern, Hangee Uppe, and She-Nannigan's House of Beer. The Lodge Tavern opened in 1957, across the street from the future Mother's.

Ryan was a bartender at the Lodge and at Mother's. "Dyed-in-the-wool Cubs fans are always at the Lodge," Ryan said. "Forever. Mother's is opposite. It's all White Sox. The irony is Mother's is on the north side of the street and the Lodge is on the south side of the street. Mother's is more blue collar. Sports announcer Harry Caray? He hit every bar on the strip: Butch's, McGuire's, the Lodge, and here."

Harry Caray was all about excess. If he had looked a little deeper he would have enjoyed the excess in disco, such as Donna Summer's 1975 orgasmic "Love to Love You Baby," the first disco song to take up an entire side of an album. The song's producer and co-writer Giorgio Moroder pioneered the kick drum on each beat of the song, which became known as "four on the floor."

Longtime Chicago rock radio personality Mitch Michaels said, "Disco music didn't bother me that much. I went to some [disco] clubs, but it was more to pick up chicks and get laid. There were a bunch of disco clubs on Mannheim Road. Disco came from soul music. It is kind of a natural progression in some ways. Look at the Motown bands of the 1960s, those guys were up there in matching silk suits with three or four gals singing in flashy dresses. It is all part of show business."

The popular Rush Street disco Faces was a private club with a door guy that had up to 16,000 card-carrying members. Faces was Chicago's best known discotheque from 1971 until it closed in 1989. People danced all night under clouds of cigarette smoke, bubbles, and mist from a fog machine.

"You had to be a member," said Michaels. "But I could get in there periodically. In 1975, part of Led Zeppelin's tour was based out of Chicago. The Zeppelin airplane was parked at O'Hare. I got off the air one night at 1:30 in the morning. A couple of buddies and I are having cocktails at Faces, and I turn to my right and Robert Plant is standing next to me having a drink, and we chatted for five or ten minutes. That's my favorite recollection of Faces."

Chicagoan Clinton Ghent hosted "Soul Train" from 1971 until 1979, replacing Don Cornelius, who relocated to Los Angeles. "There were only three black people in Chicago who had memberships to Faces," Ghent told me for a 2009 *Chicago Sun-Times* interview. "Me, Dr. Nate Clark, and Don Cornelius. I'm not bragging on myself, but I did The Hustle so great that Jimmy Rittenberg tried to get me to teach The Hustle. Disco did bring up the pay scale for artists."

Jim Rittenberg was general manager and emcee of Faces. The Chicago native helped design the club as an upscale joint to take a date after dinner, offering a more sophisticated scene than the Division Street bars just north of Faces. Rittenberg worked with the White Sox to host "Disco Nights" before Disco Demolition.

A 1979 White Sox program promoted an upcoming game with the Seattle Mariners: "The Seattle series opens Monday night, June 18, and it will feature a twenty-minute rugby game featuring Chicago's finest women ruggers. June 19 will be Disco Night, with a dance contest preceding the game . . . "

"We had twenty [raised] platforms that night," Rittenberg recalled over lunch at Gibson's on Rush Street, just a block north from the former Faces. "Each platform was about twelve-by-eight feet. They started to the right and left of home plate and went out into right and left field so everyone could see. We started with twenty couples. They were all dressed up disco style. People cheered and we had judges. We already had one contest to screen the dancers. Between our judges and applause we narrowed it down. I don't remember who the hell won. It was pretty well received. They drew around 17,000, [maybe] 20,000.

"People forget *Saturday Night Fever* was inspired by Faces," Rittenberg continued. "Studio 54 [in New York City] didn't open until 1978 or '79 and they closed in '81. We opened up years before and stayed open years after. We got everybody they got, plus Sinatra, Bob Hope, Norman Mailer, and Gore Vidal. Bonnie Swearingen [wife of late Chicago Amoco oil executive John Swearingen] would bring them in. We'd open at nine o'clock and she'd go, 'Could you do the fog for Mr. Mailer?'"

Rittenberg, born and raised in West Garfield Park, was a White Sox season ticket holder. Mike Veeck called Rittenberg about the disco dance contest. He was all in. "To me, Mike

Jimmy Rittenberg and Tom Dreesen

Veeck, Steve Dahl, and Jimmy De Castro [the former WLUP general manager who didn't arrive in Chicago until 1981] are the three best promo guys ever," Rittenberg said. "Jeff Schwartz was sharp; he was a good promoter, too. But I didn't care. I did disco, big bands, country western, rock 'n' roll. You may not order a steak, order the fish. Music was our menu, not our way of life. But Steve took it on as a movement. He destroyed disco. We started playing Harold Melvin & the Blue Notes' "The Love I Lost" in 1973 at Faces. We played it when the bands went on break and it filled the dance floor. In 1976 it filled the dance floor. In 1978 it became known from soul to disco and filled the dance floor. After disco died in 1981, we played the same song for several more years. We called it 'dance music'. Then we started playing 'My Sharona' [The Knack's 1979 hit] and Michael Jackson stuff. Steve destroyed the whole aura of disco. It happened to us, but it didn't knock us out of business. It made us sharper."

After hosting a disco dance contest just a month before what became known as Disco Demolition, Rittenberg was surprised by the turnout for the WLUP event.

"I was flabbergasted. I knew Steve Dahl had a huge following from the abuse we took. His fans walked by Faces and said 'disco sucks.' My nephew was a busboy at Faces and he couldn't even tell his friends he worked there. I used to own a part of the Park West [the Lincoln Park nightclub]. Teenage Radiation opened for [comic] Gallagher one night and Gallagher was so pissed. Nobody was there to see him. He's sort of a soft talker and the crowd is yelling, "Coho! Coho! [a reference to Dahl's Insane Coho Lips]. I was afraid of Steve's crowd.

"I did Jukebox Saturday Night and got involved with a Friday afternoon [1984 post-game] Chuck Berry concert. We did a hula hoop contest as they were setting up the stage. [Chicago Blackhawks President and CEO] John McDonough had just started there." The Cubs were struggling with attendance and post-game concerts was a device to draw more fans and keep them in the ball park.

"But with Mike Veeck, how far does the apple fall from the tree? And I idolized Bill [Veeck], so I jumped at a disco dance contest. At that time, they drew as much as the Cubs."

In 1979 the White Sox drew 1,280,702 fans, tenth out of fourteen American League teams. The Cubs drew 1,648,587 fans, sixth out of twelve National League teams.

Former Rush Street bartender Jay Emerich founded Faces in 1971. The name came from the posters slathered on the walls—slides of customers, animals, kids, and athletes. At first, Faces booked live pop and show bands seven days a week, like Iguana and New Era. Faces had a strict dress code: no jeans, no leather jacket, and a collared shirt. A suit was not mandatory.

"Faces was always about a dress code," said Rittenberg. "Clothes do not the man make, but it does say how much money you can spend. If I wasn't a minor owner at the beginning, I wouldn't have been allowed in."

Emerich contracted lupus and sold his interest to George Shlaes in 1977. After the sale, Rittenberg became general manager, known as the tuxedoed emcee with the endless smile.

"Jay was the visionary and operator," Rittenberg said. "I was the marketer. He worked through me. Its all about marketing and promotion. Nothing starts until somebody brings in the sale. We had a lot of fun. When *Star Wars* came out we had Darth Vaders running around. What is that? Promotion and marketing. What

In the late 1970s, a lifetime membership at Faces started at fifty dollars. Comps were given to Hugh Hefner, Mayor Richard M. Daley, and other big shooters who had lots of money. Customers could buy a one night membership on a slow Sunday or Monday. "We had a fifty dollar a year renewal," explained Jim Rittenberg, the face of Faces. "We'd renew at about 48 percent. We had 16,000 people and maybe 4,000 were freebies. In those days, that was a really good cut. The dress code kept out the Lincoln Avenue people and brought in the car dealers and their guys. You got a suit on and you're looking good, you're acting good."

were they doing at Sox park? The same thing. We had a lot of record parties. Donna Summer released a record there. Bands came in; the Average White Band. Chicago. John Travolta and Olivia Newton John. Brooke Shields underage, David Copperfield underage. We served Artis Gilmore [he played center for the Bulls], we didn't kick him out like BBC [the Division Street dance club] did. O.J. [Simpson] was in during the sporting goods show every winter and he behaved himself. Lou Piniella. Mickey Mantle was in with Billy Martin a couple of times. Tommy Lasorda was a regular. Old timers who knew me and Jay from our bartending days like [Orioles third baseman] Brooks Robinson."

The disco-era trifecta was Jay's, Sweetwater, and Harry's Cafe.

"Now they call it the Viagra Triangle," Rittenberg said. "[Gibson's Bar & Steakhouse on Rush) was Mister Kelly's [from 1957 to '75] so a lot of the celebrities would come to Faces. We were post-Harvey Wallbanger. We were Tequila Sunrise. Watermelon shots were big. We did a lot of promotions, like *M*A*S*H* vodka when *M*A*S*H* came out [in 1972]. Former Faces coat room attendant Kathy O'Malley is now a managing partner of Gibson's.

Pop-disco star Barry Manilow did his first TV special at Faces for *Soundstage*. Manilow had just come out with "Mandy," his 1978 hit ballad. Faces barricaded Rush Street so Manilow could run outside and sing his 1975 hit "It's a Miracle" with the hook line "dancing in the street." Faces club members joined Manilow outside.

Rittenberg added, "[Soundstage producer] Kenny Ehrlich put me in touch with Murray Allen of Universal Recording Studios, who did our sound system." Allen, who died of liver cancer in 2006, went on to collaborate with Ehrlich as sound designer for the Grammy Awards. In 1951, Universal Recording Studios, located not far from Faces, was the first studio in the country to have stereo sound. Allen recorded most of the *Vee-Jay* record catalog plus hits like Gene Chandler's "The Duke of Earl," Dee Clark's "Hey Little Girl," and John Lee Hooker's "Boom Boom."

And then Rittenberg was interrupted.

Comic Tom Dreesen walked up to Rittenberg's table at Gibson's. Dreesen was in town to throw out the first pitch at a Cubs-Dodgers game. "Faces was *the* place to go," said Dreesen, who was a longtime opening act for Frank Sinatra. "If you wanted to get laid, Jimmy had the hottest looking girls. And I never worked blue. When disco became hot, like anybody else you went where the girls were. I liked Sinatra and Johnny Mathis, but I'd get on the dance floor and pretend I knew what I was doing. Fortunately, the floor was so crowded nobody could tell if you could dance. Sinatra hated disco."

Dreesen knew Rittenberg as far back as 1969, when Dreesen worked at Mister Kelly's and would adjourn to Punchinello's bar on Rush Street. Dreesen began opening for Frank Sinatra in 1982. "Jimmy Rittenberg was what Rush Street was all about," Dreesen said. "A promoter. Smart. Good friends all around who were willing to support him."

Working class hero Jim Petrerik (Ides of March, Survivor) also looks back at Faces with a rich smile.

"My main Faces memory was when Chase put out their *Pure Music* record," said Peterik. The Chicago-based, jazz-rock fusion band released *Pure Music* in 1974 on Epic Records, a follow-up to their 1971 self-titled debut album that delivered the hard-driving hit single "Get It On."

"I sang and wrote two songs ['Run Back to Mama,' with bandleader and trumpet player Bill Chase, and 'Love Is On the Way'] on *Pure Music*," Peterik recalled. "The record company sponsored a promotional tour. I played the Cellar Door in New York City, Los Angeles, and then Faces with Chase. The place was packed. It was sad because at the end Bill [Chase] said, 'You're going to see a lot more of me writing with Jim Peterik.' About three weeks later his plane went down and almost all the band members were killed."

Bill Chase died on August 9, 1974, when a chartered Piper Win Comanche crashed en route to a concert in Jackson, Minnestoa. Keyboardist Wally Yohn, drummer Walter Clark, and guitarist John Emma were also killed, along with the pilot Daniel Ludwig and co-pilot Linda Swisher. "I was supposed to be on that plane," Peterik said. "I had a solo show and couldn't make it. I had a little bit of survivor's guilt, and it actually is one of the main reasons I named our new band Survivor.

Dennis DeYoung of Styx never went to Faces.

"Naw," he declared. "We did go to the opening of the Limelight [in 1985]. There's a picture of me, Andy Warhol, and Tony Bennett. Can you believe that? Never went to Faces. I wasn't that guy. I dance with my wife in my house. Would you go to a disco if you had a wife?"

DeYoung and his wife Suzanne did go to a New York disco in 1987 when he produced a couple of tracks for Liza Minnelli. "She stayed at my house," he said. "We recorded her at Pumpkin [Studios]. Gene Simmons called me up and said he was trying to get a record deal for Liza. He said, 'I want you to coach her into being a pop singer.' I met her in New York. The tracks were never released but she did great. I think the demos were used to get the Pet Shop Boys to produce an album for her. Liza is a good human being, right to the core. She took us to a disco and we hung out.

"The new wave bands came in and a lot of them had dance rhythm structure to their music. People kept dancing, they just didn't call it disco anymore. Even now, everything rocks except rock. Think about it. So how do they rise above this? By wearing a meat dress, which is counter productive because Lady Gaga is really fucking good! But Lady Gaga knows what Dahl knew: I'm going to blow up records. What Springsteen knew: I'm going to tear my jeans in the right place. You gotta have a gimmick. That's all it is."

Like Rittenberg, Chicago sportscaster Les Grobstein's roots are in gritty Garfield Park, but in 1979 he was living in a townhouse in unincorporated Des Plaines. "I went to disco clubs a couple times," he admitted. "I don't drink alcohol. I don't smoke. I don't do drugs. I'm proud to say I'm very square. I didn't realize I'd be working for WLS later in 1979, but I remember listening to 'My Sharona,' which was number one. 'We are Family' by Sister Sledge became the theme song for the Pittsburgh Pirates. [The late Pirates slugger] Willie Stargell played it on his boom box after games."

The Metro's Joe Shanahan did not listen to commercial disco and dance during the hey-day of Faces. "It wasn't a life I lived," Shanahan said. "*Saturday Night Fever* was popular in the straight and gay discos. The Bee Gees. Yvonne Elliman. But even that record had some of those songs, like a disco cover of 'The 1812 Overture?' That's just wrong on so many levels. You don't want to dance to that. You want to dance to the gritty funk of the Ohio Players. There were labels in New York birthing a sound like 99 Records that had punk-disco bands like ESG and Liquid Liquid. That's where our heads were at. That was the blueprint for hip-hop, just as Kraftwerk was a blueprint for Afrika Bambatta and Soulsonic Force. What was great about all that is that the line was blurred between black and white and gay and straight.

"I sensed there was a division with the freak flag of the Dahl demolition. I'm walking down Clark Street and someone leans out the door because I have a short punk rock haircut and they call me a faggot. I said, 'What? Because I look like this?' They were out looking to beat up people. I got it. I'm a South Sider. I come to the North Side because there's a definite dividing line."

South Side native Darlene Jackson (DJ Lady D) is a producer and owner of the D'lectable Music label. She has played house music at Chicago's Lollapalloza music festival and performed sets of disco and techno in Asia and Europe.

In conversation at a Ukrainian Village coffee shop, she spoke of the ethnomusicological dividing line between house and disco.

"Disco had its own look. They had a fashion to disco. House had a fashion. The disco beat had a high ride click-click-click that was always present. In house it turned into a bit of a shuffle. You get the syncopation between the kick drums, bass drums, the snare, and the high hat. They're both 4/4. The art of mixing continued off from disco into house, but it got a lot more complex. Many more tricks and effects to make the experience even more trippy than disco.

"My jump off point was house music, and a community of people started house. It was gay people. From where I was, you didn't express homophobia, because you could look to the left or right of you and see someone gay. Or someone who appeared to be gay but wasn't out. There wasn't a lot of saying certain things or calling people names. I'm sure some of that went on, but if you were in the house you were in the house. You did not talk about who else was in the house. We knew it had its origins in disco. And a lot of early house parties were playing disco sets. It was more unacceptable to not accept all that. You'd go to a club, like LaRays or C.O.D., that was popular in the 1980s—there were drag queens there. We were all one community."

"I remember [Disco Demolition] photographically in my mind," said Shanahan in soft tones. "I had an apartment on Wells Street in Old Town. I was tending bar and waiting tables. I was doing my own little after hours parties in my loft and other locations. I was very close to Jim [Nash] and Dannie [Flesher] from Wax Trax! They were openly gay. We went to that club on Wells Street where Jeffrey Dahmer picked up guys. I'm trying to think of the club now. [It was Carol's Speakeasy at 1355 North Wells]. A footnote: We would go there to hear Frankie Knuckles spin. He had a residency there on a Thursday night. Frankie would play the rhythmic pieces, the Talking Heads. So when Jim and Dannie opened Wax Trax! (on North Lincoln Avenue in 1978), they didn't have a disco section so to speak, but they had music that was rhythmic. Duran Duran sounded like a Giorgio Moroder disco record. Human League. Spandau Ballet. Those bands had a rhythm to it. Some of it was bad, some of it was good. But that wasn't music we actually wanted to listen to."

Shanahan wasn't a fan of the commercialization of disco, noting Memphis DJ Rick Dees' 1976 number one novelty hit "Disco Duck." Shanahan said, "I thought that was a bastardization of a great, true genre of music that actually was super liberating for so many people. It got people dancing. It was a communal activity of release. That was fantastic."

Chicago chef and fifth generation Bridgeport resident Kevin Hickey attended Disco Demolition. He reflected, "I would almost attribute the instant backlash from Disco Demolition [as] helping seal disco's fate in America. Bam. It was done. I was young but I remember that overnight after that event you were unbelievably uncool. Then with costumes, goofiness, and novelty songs like 'Disco Duck' it killed itself as well." Hickey is no relation to White Sox pitcher Kevin Hickey (1956–2012). "I met him at a charity event a few years before he passed," Hickey said. "Nicest guy in the world. The only time we had an issue was when I would call him. It would be like Abbott and Costello's 'Who's on First.' I'd be, 'Kevin, this is Kevin Hickey.' He'd go this is 'Kevin Hickey,' and I'd say 'Kevin, this is me, Kevin.' Then he'd stop listening to me."

Dahl said, "I went once to Faces but it was after it was on the way out. It may have been because Dan Aykroyd was making *Doctor Detroit* there. Was the Smart Bar disco? Is that why Joe [Shanahan] hates me? I used

Darlene "DJ Lady D" Jackson

to go there and get fucked up. I don't remember it being a disco or anything. There were a lot of rock clubs that were switching to disco. I guess there was more money in that.

"I think there's a novelty resurgence in disco now in theme parties, stuff like that. I'd say it came back in house or EDM of some form. All that seems more accessible now. Any of us could go to a club now and take molly," Dahl laughs. "It's not so out of reach for everybody. I guess it's how culture progresses. I wouldn't have known how to go to a club and wear a suit. I wouldn't know what to do. There was a lot of intimidation and disenfranchisement, especially if you were a male."

In July of 1979 Chuck Renslow of "Man's Country" fame ran the gay club Center Stage, where Metro is now. STAGES followed Center Stage. Jim McNamara and Bob Rudnick opened STAGES after having some success at Tuts in the former Quiet Knight on West Belmont.

Shanahan used to guest deejay on punk nights at NEO.

"I'd play this hybrid of punk rock, Prince, and this dirtier Parliament stuff," Shanahan said. "The owner told me I was ruining his club. He said, 'Take this music off. We're a new wave club.' I said, 'You can't tell me what to play. Look at your dance floor. It's full.' He said the music was going to draw a 'bad element' and he didn't want it to become a 'black club.' Now, [I thought] 'Smart Bar has to open.' It was 1979 or '80 and took me a little time to find the building to do it in, but that was the era. I basically got fired for playing black music in a white club."

Disco is on the cusp of entering the age of ironic nostalgia. It may not be long before you see KC and the Sunshine Band appearing at Pitchfork Music Festival.

Former WLUP promotions director Dave Logan pointed out, "During Disco Demolition, all the media available was fifteen radio stations. That was the world. Today there's fifteen disco stations online that we can find from the satellite on the phone in thirty seconds. When we launched XM Satellite radio, we had a disco channel and it was huge. A lot of people liked what it was. And for a lot of people, disco represented a good time on a Saturday night, dancing. Women particularly liked it. It was fun once you got past the Studio 54 image."

Disco also took gigs away from live rock 'n' roll bands. It was cheaper for a club owner to bring in a turntable and DJ than hire a live band, a soundman, and sometimes a crew.

In the wake of disco, Joe Shanahan turned Metro into one of the premiere live music clubs in America. "A lot of musicians felt they weren't getting enough work because clubs were doing more dance nights or whatever," Shanahan said. "Those bands were bad. Off Broadway was working their asses off. We'd go see them all the time. The Hounds. Cheap Trick. That was tougher urban rock 'n' roll. It wasn't Journey or the Eagles. I wasn't into bad metal. I was more into power pop like Pez Band. Mother's was doing shows then."

In the late 1970s, Wax Trax! owners were independently booking acts like the Jam at Mother's. In its nascent years, Mother's booked acts like Eric Clapton with Cream and Lou Reed with the Velvet Underground. (The club still has a guitar autographed by Reed.)

Owner Gorsuch was a healthy seventy-eight years old in the spring of 2015. "Honestly I don't remember the Velvet Underground," said Gorsuch, whose first Chicago bartending gig was in 1964 at The Store, which was in the former folk club Gate of Horn on Rush and Oak Streets. He then asked, "Do you know how to stop sex after fifty? Take your clothes off."

Jam Production co-founder Jerry Mickelson remembered, "We were booking Molly Hatchet, Journey, Van Halen, Yes, Genesis, Marshall Tucker, Lou Reed. The number of [live] disco bands never came close to rock bands. You had Donna Summer. The Bee Gees. They came into the headline arena level. We produced shows by Gloria Gaynor. The Village People. KC and the Sunshine Band. The Trammps. The Ohio Players. Gino Vannelli. Was Barry White disco?"

Veeck said, "Over the years people have given me hundreds of mementos. Scorched records. That's their idea of real fun. I come to do a speaking engagement and they go, 'Here's something you haven't seen!' And I have to thank them. I will say the last one, [my wife] Libby and I went to the Atlantic League All-Star game and both teams signed a Donna Summer record, which was very funny."

Nile Rodgers and Bernard Edwards of CHIC and David Bowie at the Frankie Crocker Awards at the Savoy in New York City on January 21, 1983. Photo by Ebet Roberts.

10. NILE RODGERS GOOD TIMES

Maybe Nile Rodgers doesn't have the crossover home run with David Bowie without Disco Demolition . . .

D isco Demolition put the hammer down on bad disco music, but the soul-funk dance band Chic endured with "Good Times," a number one hit in the summer of 1979.

The Disco Demolition fallout also caught up with Rodgers. Chic would never have another hit. Outside of producing Sister Sledge, a 1980 Diana Ross project, and collaborating with crooner Johnny Mathis, Rodgers could not find steady work until 1983, when he met David Bowie and produced *Let's Dance*, which delivered the hit single, "Modern Love" and "China Girl." Rodgers introduced Bowie to a younger crossover generation.

Rodgers went on to produce Duran Duran, Daft Punk, Lady Gaga, Pharrell Williams, and Keith Urban. Plus, Chic's fingerprints are all over Madonna's smash 1984 album *Like a Virgin*. Rodgers and his late songwriting partner Bernard Edwards are ten-time nominees to the Rock and Roll Hall of Fame. The heavenly jazz-rock guitar of Rodgers and the hell-deep bass playing of Edwards illuminated a nocturnal generation.

"We were in Europe when the Disco Demolition thing was happening," Rodgers said in a March 2016 interview from New York. "The way it looked for us, it was, well, this was also during the time of ABA [rogue American Basketball Association], so we were into people having big pranks and tricks. The magnitude of entertainment at these events seemed funny to me. We weren't offended and we didn't think they were talking about us.

"But when we got home it was made overly apparent that not only were they talking about us, but they had pitted this group called the Knack against Chic. The Knack were our friends. The Knack were going to be the saviors of rock 'n' roll and Chic were dark lords of the underworld trying to keep the four chord rockers from having their rightful fortune of millions of dollars. I started out in four chord rock bands. There was a time where I could only play four chords."

Rodgers was born September 19, 1952 in New York City. His biological mother was fourteen at the time, and she gave him up for adoption, but they were reunited within a year. Rodgers' first professional gig was at nineteen, as a musician in the Sesame Street touring band. "I was a movie fanatic and loved the Marx Brothers," he said. "I read the [1974] book *Harpo Speaks*, by Harpo Marx, the brother who pretends to be mute. He told of leaving school at nine years old to get a job. He became a musical virtuoso. I said, 'I want to be like him'." After Sesame Street, Rodgers's next stop was to join the house band at the legendary Apollo Theater in Harlem, where he backed Aretha Franklin and Parliament-Funkadelic.

"Disco Demolition caught us completely by surprise until we started to try and interact with record executives and people who had been our friends," Rodgers said. "People weren't answering our phone calls. It happens once or twice, you go, 'Well, I guess the person's pretty busy.' But then it's, 'I just made a few million dollars for this guy, what's going on?' And then the 'Disco sucks' thing became very real. It was scary. We were in the middle of a contract with Diana Ross and we got the contract signed—thank God—and we realized we had to change our musical style on our first record we were doing with a big superstar. Unbeknownst to her, when we take on an assignment we do everything. We write the songs. I do all the orchestration. It was like her moving into another Motown."

The result was Ross's 1980 release *Diana* for Motown Records that delivered the smash hits "Upside Down" and the up-tempo gay anthem "I'm Coming Out." Motown was a label known for hit singles, but it released the album without one.

Diana was Ross's final project for Motown.

"Funny things happened in 1979," Rodgers reflected. "A number of unusual events collided at the same time. Prior to that event, what was disco culture like? All over the world, clubs tried to emulate the disco mentality, most famously Studio 54. People were very open sexually. Men could go to the girl's bathroom, vice-versa. People were transgender and everybody felt comfortable. This was amazing. This felt more political than hippies, Black Panthers, or anything I had been involved in. This was the world I wanted to live in, where everybody was cool with everyone. You were respectful. That was because of the music."

"Good Times" was released in June, 1979, a month before Disco Demolition. It sold more than five million copies, making it the best selling 45 single in the history of Atlantic Records at the time. "Good Times" is one of the most sampled songs in music history.

Rodgers recalled, "[Chic] had two number one pop disco records in 1979, ['Good Times'] and 'Le Freak,' [which] wound up going number one even though it had come out the year before. And then the Pittsburgh Pirates adopted 'We are Family' (by Sister Sledge, produced by Rodgers) as their theme song, and they won the World Series. You were hearing 'We are Family' in baseball stadiums."

Work dried up, however, until 1983, when Rodgers and rocker Billy Idol went to the after-hours Continental club in New York City where they ran into David Bowie.

"Billy went, 'David Baah-wie,' that's how English people say it," Rodgers explained. "Then he barfed while he was saying 'Baah-wie.' He wiped his hand on his sleeve and said, 'Hello mate.' David and I got to talking and neither David or I had known about the other's love of jazz music. That's what linked us together forever. That's why a record like *Let's Dance* exists.

"David wrote a folk song with traditional folk changes. What you hear is what I did. I said, 'David, even though I've been running from the word 'dance' since Disco Demolition, if you are going to call a song 'Let's Dance,' you better make damn well sure people want to dance to this.' David brought Stevie Ray Vaughan to the session [to play lead guitar on "Let's Dance"]. David only knew two people when we did that record: Nile Rodgers and Stevie Ray Vaughan. He had never met everybody else who played on that record." Artists such as Luther Vandross and Carlos Alomar appeared on Bowie's 1975 *Young Americans* album. They went to the same high school as Rodgers.

In July 2016, Chic appeared with the Brit pop band Duran Duran in a two-night concert at the popular Ravinia Festival in Highland Park, a world away from Comiskey Park. "Duran Duran is my second band," Rodgers said. "They feel like Chic Lite to me. They came into my life during the whole 'Disco sucks' era and I was able to do my first records

TEN ESSENTIAL NILE RODGERS TRACKS

1. "Le Freak," Chic, 1978
2. "I'm Coming Out," Diana Ross, 1980 (later sampled by Notorious BIG)
3. "I'm Not Perfect," Grace Jones, 1986
4. "Let's Dance," David Bowie, 1983
5. "Like a Virgin," Madonna, 1984
6. "Get Lucky," Daft Punk and Pharrell Williams, 2013
7. "Good Times, Chic, 1979 (a cornerstone riff for The Sugarhill Gang)
8. "We Are Family," Sister Sledge, 1979
9. "Backfired," Debbie Harry, 1981
10. "Dance, Dance, Dance (Yowza, Yowza, Yowza)," Chic, 1977

Honorable mention: "It's Alright to Love Me," Johnny Mathis, 1981 with them as part of their band." (Rodgers remixed the hit studio track "The Wild Boys" from Duran Duran's 1984 *Arena* album.) Rodgers continued, "Their newest album, which has been their biggest hit in thirty-two years, is the first album I've done with them in thirty-two years. Do you think there's a correlation?"

Steve Dahl with fans at Disco Demolition

Harry Wayne Casey

11. HARRY WAYNE CASEY AND KC AND THE SUNSHINE BAND— GODFATHERS OF DISCO

From the mid- to late-1970s, no disco group was as commercially successful as KC and the Sunshine Band. Chic were savants at crossing over into funk, soul, and rock. KC and the Sunshine band took disco from the sweaty nightclub into the daylight. In the summer of 2015, KC and the Sunshine Band attracted a large crowd to the Indiana State Fair, and for some young members of the audience there was an ironic twist in watching the band perform. Could disco be poised for a comeback?

Before he boogied into a set with KC and the Sunshine Band that sparkled with disco ball nostalgia, the band's founding singer Harry Wayne Casey looked out at the crowd at the Indiana State Fair. "I'm sixty-four," Casey said on a cool night in August 2015. "I can't even remember if that's the way I like it."

The summer of 2015 marked the fortieth anniversary of KC and the Sunshine Band's biggest commercial breakthrough with hits "Get Down Tonight," "That's the Way (I Like It)," "Shake Shake Shake (Shake Your Booty)," and "Keep It Comin' Love." In 1975, KC and the Sunshine Band became the first group since the Beatles to have four number one pop songs in a twelve-month period, and they accomplished the feat with a unique blend of dance music, reggae, and Bahamas Junkanoo that filtered through Casey's native South Florida. KC and the Sunshine Band were a Sunshine State version of Tavares, the popular mid-1970s, soul-funk brothers of Cape Verdean descent who grew up in Rhode Island.

Then disco happened.

Casey remembers Disco Demolition.

"Although I'm the godfather and one of the main creators of the whole thing, by that time I was not what disco had become," Casey said in a pre-show conversation at his hotel in downtown Indianapolis. "By 1979, I had 'Please Don't Go' (the band's first ballad) and 'Yes, I'm Ready' (another ballad), both number one records.

"Evidently Disco Demolition didn't do anything. Because it's bigger than ever. It just changed its name from 'disco' to 'new wave.' You couldn't be more disco than Madonna. That was dance music reinvented more electronically (by Nile Rodgers and Bernard Edwards). Demolition did nothing but get rid of a word I didn't like to begin with.

Casey kept it coming on.

He continued, "What's crazy about Disco Demolition is that everybody thought it was world wide. It happened in one place, in Chicago, in a field with 600 people or whatever. They didn't do that in Miami. They didn't do it in LA or New York. Because of the press, you thought the whole world was burning disco records. People are afraid of change. We changed the sound [just] like Elvis changed the sound in the fifties and the Beatles did in the sixties. We almost got rid of a whole genre of rock music."

As early as 1965, *The Tonight Show* bandleader Skitch Henderson recorded "Skitch Plays The Mule/And Discotheque Selections" in a promotional album for the Smirnoff Mule. In part, the liner notes read, "When 'Killer Joe' Piro, King of the Discotheque, introduced The Mule as a new departure in dancing, the action started. Suddenly a new hit tune, 'The Mule' swept across the nation. Then from the dance and tune a new drink became popular with America's Discotheque society . . . "

Casey reflected, "Disco didn't make sense. I thought the seventies was the breakthrough of R&B music, if anything else. They renamed it disco and it took that glory away. R&B wasn't as important as pop—and now it was more important than pop. Let's just bury it and call it disco. That pissed me off. I didn't really want to have any association with it."

Casey was an architect of "Sunshine Soul" at T.K. Records in Miami, Florida, whose umbrella covered independent labels like Marlin, Alston, and Stone Dog. T.K. are the initials of sound engineer Terry Kane, who built a small eight-track recording studio in the building's offices in Hialeah, Florida.

But the T.K. label itself received national attention with Peter Brown's 1977 disco hit "Do Ya Wanna Get Funky With Me," the stark 1972 Timmy Thomas smash "Why Can't We Live Together," and Anita Ward's 1979 disco hit "Ring My Bell." Casey and his collaborator Richard Finch wrote the 1974 George McRae hit "Rock Your Baby," which Casey covered at the Indiana State Fair, and in 1977, KC and the Sunshine Band recorded "I'm Your Boogie Man" at the studio. In 1980, James Brown even resurfaced at T.K., cutting "Rapp Payback (Where Iz Moses)." The Godfather of Soul became a mentor to the unwilling Godfather of Disco.

"He would come in all the time," Casey said. "He was 'Mr. Brown.' I was in the inner circle, so I would be around him more than anyone else there. Besides doing some backgrounds, sessions, and co-writing, I managed some artists, I did PR, promotion. Working in the stockroom. What ever was available to do that day, I just kept myself occupied. There was nothing I didn't know about the business. I did very well in every department I worked in.

"But I wasn't going to get discovered."

Casey said his artistic break came when he attended the wedding of T.K. to R&B vocalist Betty Wright— although other sources said he attended the wedding of the late Clarence Henry Reid, the seminal rapper known as "Blowfly."

"Clarence was the main writer for T.K.," said Casey. "He wrote Betty Wright's first record when she was thirteen, 'Girls Can't Do What Guys Do and Still Be a Lady.' He wrote [the 1971 smash hit] 'Clean Up Woman.' He wrote 'Rockin' Chair' for Gwen McRae. Then he became Blowfly, who plagiarized everyone's songs and did filthy, dirty versions of them." (For example, Blowfly turned songwriter Stanley Adams's "What a Difference a Day Makes" into "What a Difference a Lay Makes.")

Unfortunately, Adams was ASCAP president at the time, and he sued Reid.

"Betty hired a Junkanoo band," Casey recalled, referring to the popular street band from Belize and the Bahamas that relies on bells, steel drums, and whistles. "The music was so infectious, I thought it would be great to put it on record. I was managing Timmy Thomas at the time. We did a show in Washington, DC. Earth, Wind and Fire was headlining. The audience had whistles. I remembered the Junkanoo band had whistles, cowbells, and horns. It was so intense. I thought, 'I need to make a record of this.' So I went in the studio with some musicians, brought in a Junkanoo band and wrote 'Blow Your Whistle.' I named it KC and the Sunshine Junkanoo Band. But it really was just me."

Casey grew up in the Miami-Dade County area, where his mother had a record collection that included Ray Charles, the Flamingos, and Nancy Wilson. As he came of age, he danced at Miami discos. He also caught Wayne Cochran frenetic concerts. The pompadoured Cochran was the white man's James Brown, and Cochran recorded for Brown's King label. "There was a place called The Place and a place called The World," Casey said. "The World was an old blimp hangar. It had two stages on each end, and that's where we'd see Wayne Cochran. He tore the place apart. He would climb the rafters. I've never seen such a show in my life. I was seventeen, eighteen years old. Besides James Brown, I don't think there was a better performer." Cochran is now an evangelist in the Miami area.

The summer of 1975 was good to Casey; it launched his career, which now allows him to take a fifteen-piece band on the road (including four dancers) like he did for the Indiana State Fair. Looking a bit like Billy Crystal, he fronted the band with a casino-type shtick. He told the audience, "I was your mother's *NSYNC."

As Casey leaned back on a hotel lobby sofa, he said, "The mid-1970s were exciting because T.K. was pretty much a one-hit record label. After I had the George McRae record, all of a sudden I had 'Get Down Tonight.' Then 'That's The Way I Like It,' and I seemed to break the curse. I was the only one at T.K. that ever managed to do that. I just took off from that original Caribbean Junkanoo sound."

Some disco historians maintain the mega disco success of KC and the Sunshine Band squeezed African-American artists off the charts. "Oh, why do people even go there," he groaned. "If I did anything, I opened it up not only for black artists but for white artists world wide. I helped break down all those barriers. We made it acceptable for everybody. We were right there to finally say, 'You know what. It's okay. Prejudice doesn't need to exist in the music industry.'"

KC and the Sunshine Band were the first large interracial group to break through to a mass audience in television and film. "Boogie Shoes" wound up on the soundtrack album for "*Saturday Night Fever*, as did the Tavares' hit "More Than a Woman."

Three Dog Night had a black drummer," Casey said, referring to Floyd Sneed, formerly of the Tommy Chong Band. "I can't say we were the first one, but our music was first of a mixed type of situation to be on R&B and the pop charts."

Casey left the T.K. camp in 1976, but the hits kept coming. He collaborated with Teri DeSario on her 1979 hit "Yes I'm Ready" when T.K. began winding down. Some T.K. artists weren't as empathetic as Casey. In 1980, southern soul singer Latimore cut "Discoed to Death." Weird Al Yankovic's "Another One Rides the Bus," was the final T.K. single in 1980. T.K. went out of business in 1981.

"I'm not sure how much was actually recorded at T.K," Casey said. "Foxy [the Latin dance band from Hialeah, Florida] may have been. Most things that were recorded were sent to T.K. at the time."

Casey said T.K. only occupied a small portion of a 100,000-square foot building. Bronx, New York born Henry Stone was the key player in the operation. As early as 1948, Stone was distributing records in Miami, and he was an early champion of James Brown. In 1956, Stone worked with Federal Records (a subsidiary of King) to "Please Please Please" as the soul king's first action on the charts. Casablanca and T.K. Records pioneered the twelve-inch disco single, a format still used today.

"Henry was the largest independent distributor in southeast America," Casey said. "He was responsible for Atlantic, Warner Brothers, Reprise, Motown, Stax, Chess, Checker, MGM, everything but RCA and Columbia. If you wanted a record, you got it directly from Henry. All those records would come through our building. This was up until 1971, '72. Once Warner Brothers and Atlantic decided to become WEA, we started boxing all those records up and shipping them out. We were told we would no longer be the distributor, and they were forming their own distribution arm. Then it happened to MGM, Dunhill. It never happened with Motown, and Stax stayed the same. But that was the beginning of the record industry becoming corporate."

The state fair crowd enjoyed Casey's self-effacing humor as he riffed on his weight gain, calling his act "KFC and the Sunshine Band." And besides loving the disco classics, the audience danced to Casey's 1984 punchy pop hit "Give It Up," which hit number one in the United Kingdom.

Casey recorded "Give It Up" two years after he suffered a car accident that left him temporarily paralyzed. It took Casey nearly a year to relearn how to dance and play the keyboards.

"'Give it Up' came to me in the hospital bed," he said. "It's not 'give it up' sex-wise, it is about [how] I've always been after the person that didn't want me, or someone that everyone wanted. I couldn't find the person that just needed someone. Everybody wants your love, but I just want to make you mine all mine. It's funny, I wrote that in 1983 and then I did give it up and retire. I was done. I was fried. I was over it. I was disgusted by the industry. I was saddened by it. I wanted to bring it to a zero."

Casey got back in the game in 1991 when Arsenio Hall asked KC and the Sunshine Band to reunite for his television show. "Once I did the show I realized I missed this," he said. "I started doing some dates, just me and the girls doing stuff to track. There was an incredible response. Everywhere we went, we were packed. I had James Brown in one ear asking why I wasn't out there making music. So I started taking shows; meanwhile, I am as high as a kite. I never missed a show but I made a decision, this or career. It was career. And I went to rehab for three months."

Casey was still making music in 2015, releasing a collection of 1960s covers called *Feeling You! The 60's* that included his takes on soul standards like "You've Really Got a Hold On Me" and Aaron Neville's "Tell

It Like It Is." Casey also included a spritely version of "Blowin' In the Wind," which features the Unity On the Bay Choir from Miami.

"What a great song Bob Dylan wrote back in the sixties," Casey said. "We were going through the Vietnam War and all of that stuff. The answer is in the blowing fucking wind. How many more times are we going to bomb people? When do we say, 'What are we doing? Where is the love? Where is the compassion for people?' It was a personal song for me."

Fans wait to enter the park

Nancy Faust

12. NANCY FAUST: THE ONLY LIVE ACT THAT NIGHT

Steve and Garry's backing band Teenage Radiation was scheduled to play a short set between games of the July 12, 1979 double-header, but the band was scrapped at the last minute due to logistics. It was up to the White Sox organist to serenade the lively audience.

White Sox organist Nancy Faust thought there might be trouble between games of the Disco Demolition double-header. The typed out White Sox "Responsibility Sheet" for between game banter read, in part:

"... DAHL—AD LIB—GET READY FOR BLOW UP OF DISCO RECORDS. (LIGHT FUSE, ETC. FOR BLOWING UP OF DISCO RECORDS) (AFTER BLOWING UP DISCO RECORDS ... STEVE AND LORELEI MOVE NEXT TO HOME PLATE AREA ...) (NANCY FAUST WILL PLAY "DO YA THINK I'M SEXY") (STEVE WILL DO ... "DO YOU THINK I'M DISCO") (THANK YOUS AND CLEAR FIELD FOR SECOND GAME) ...

The field was eventually cleared, but the second game was never played.

Dahl and Faust muddled through the parody song through the smoke and the mayhem. "I never received a script like this," Faust said with a smile, looking at the 1979 pre-game sheet. We met up to chat before a Kane County Cougars game in Geneva, Illinois, where she plays organ for most Sunday home games. "Every promotion I just winged it. I remember the ethnic promotions. I had to learn the anthem for each country and that was a struggle. And the country promotions, where they would bring out cows. I probably played some disco songs before the game. I played what I thought was appropriate at the moment."

Cue Bob Seger's "The Fire Down Below."

"Had we made it to a second game, I probably would have realized you don't play disco," she said.

When Faust debuted as the White Sox organist in 1970, she was playing tunes for one of the worst teams in White Sox history. The 1970 Sox finished 59 - 103. Faust played for the 2005 World Championships before closing out her White Sox career in October 2010.

Faust didn't miss a game until 1983 when she had her son Eric.

"Bill Veeck did the unusual thing of placing the organ out with the people," said Faust, who played Old Comiskey and U.S. Cellular Field more than 3,000 times. "Before that, the organ was hidden where it would stay out of the weather. Moving it outside was to my advantage."

In 1973, Holcomb moved Faust from the center field bleachers to the upper deck, directly behind home plate. Veeck later moved her to her upper deck perch near section 234 along the third base line where she enjoyed even more interaction with thirsty White Sox fans. "One time [rock singer] Del Shannon sat next to me on the bench up there," she said. "The 'Vehicle Baby' guy? [Jim Peterik], he came up there."

Van McCoy's 1975 hit "The Hustle" was the first disco song Faust ever played. She used it every time a White Sox player hustled along the base paths.

"After that, somebody taught me how to do the dance," she said, pulling out a *Chicago Tribune* article with the headline "How To Hustle Without Hassle." She continued, "I was excited because this article was in Arts and Entertainment, yet they recognized the song at a ballgame. It made me look like I was part of the 'current scene.' I thought the timing for Disco Demolition was good, because disco had run its course by 1979. I loved disco because it lent itself so well to playing. It sounded good. I had a basic drum machine that had a disco beat. I could assign 100 beats for the songs I played. In those days I was the music. That was before technology and a DJ who could push a button for any song. That's why my drum machine was really progressive."

Faust was known for her talent in pairing a song with a player: "Disco Inferno," The Trammps' 1976 hit, for pitcher Britt Burns; "He's So Shy," The Pointer Sisters' 1980 disco-tinged hit, for the reserved outfielder Harold Baines; "Tragedy," The Bee Gees' 1979 hit, for a White Sox loss.

Faust didn't see Disco Demolition coming.

"At first I saw little fires breaking out in the outfield," she recalled. "Three nuns were sitting near me. They turned around and asked, 'What is everybody chanting?' In those days, 'Disco sucks' wasn't a nice thing to say. My friend with the tickets told them, 'They're just going, 'Let's go Sox.' But that was part of the promotion. Do you call it progressive?

"Of course when Harry [Caray] and Bill [Veeck] got on the P.A. and told people to take their seats, I stopped playing. We did try to play and sing 'Take Me Out to the Ball Game' to get people to organize in a respectful way. I realized this was getting out of hand. It was surreal. Later you analyze it and realize these weren't all baseball fans. Steve Dahl had a mixed following, and this was a great venue for them to come out and have a good time."

Faust's family history is one of a homespun good time.

Her late mother Jackie was popular in the early 1940s as part of the Jenny, Joy, and Jean act on the *WLS National Barn Dance*. (Jackie Faust was renamed Jean for the act so she wouldn't be confused with a male performer.) Jackie played accordion on the Barn Dance and wrote the melody. After that, Jackie took up the organ and played at county fairs throughout the Midwest. Her daughter would accompany her on road trips.

Faust married her husband Joe Jenkins in August 1980, but would drop into Division Street disco bars as a single woman. "Oh my goodness, I would go to a place called The Rookery," she said. "I'd go there after games once in a while. That was my place to hear disco music. And I loved it. How can you not like that beat? Even that song today, '[Get] Lucky' by Pharrell Williams, that is so disco. I found that the disco beat stayed the same but the instrumentation became different. There was more techno, but it was still dance music.

"I played all those disco songs. Everything was Top 40, unlike now where everything is categorized: adult contemporary, country, rap. I still play everything. I do songs from kid's shows because there's kids here. Last year Donna Summer died and I worked up a medley of her disco songs 'Last Dance,' and 'Dim All The Lights.' I liked disco. I never analyzed the music. Every time I learned a new song it was my favorite song."

NANCY FAUST'S DISCO PLAYLIST

"More, More, More," Andrea True Connection—for Junior Moore

"Whatcha Gonna Do," Pablo Cruz—for Henry Cruz

"Ring My Bell," Anita Ward—for Kevin Bell

"Fly Robin Fly," Silver Convention—for Robin Ventura

"Do Ya Think I'm Sexy," Rod Stewart—for Steve Sax

Steve Dahl and Lorelei Shark

144

13. LORELEI—THE ORIGINAL LOOP ROCK GIRL

Edmund Goldman helped introduce Godzilla to America. His daughter is a goddess of rock who stood alongside Steve Dahl to quell the raging fires of disco.

"Lorelei," Shark, formerly Ray, is one of the most iconic radio advertising images of the twentieth century. The bleached blonde with the tight black T-shirt was the original "Loop Rock Girl." Her rich, red lips are iconic—adorning the famous poster for *Rocky Horror Picture Show*. Yet few people know of her Hollywood lineage.

Shark was born in Manila, Philippines, moved to Japan, then Los Angeles when she was six.

She never lived in Chicago.

"Since you are who you are by the time you are six, I'm basically Asian," Shark said in a 2015 phone conversation from her home in Malibu, California. Her father Ed Goldman was head of motion picture distribution for Columbia Pictures in the Far East. "He was responsible for bringing *Godzilla* to the U.S. [in 1954]," Shark said. "When we came here from Japan in 1953, he worked with Toho [the Japanese motion picture production company] which was the MGM of Japan. He brought their product here. I did motion picture advertising after I modeled. I had my own production company [Moon Man Productions] for twenty-five years. That was fun because I'm an artist. I'm probably more of a creative being than anything else."

Shark was a professional model whose image was championed by the hormone-infused rock stations of the late 1970s. "I began doing lip things in the early 1970s," she said. "I only went into Chicago three or four times, for Loopfest. A couple of other odds and ends. And Disco Demolition."

Listeners would have been surprised to learn about Lorelei's demure home life. "I was a housewife who lived in the San Fernando Valley," she said. "People never realized I had kids. When Disco Demo happened my kids were three and six years old. I was thirty-two in 1979. Most people in 1979 thought I was twenty-two, which was funny. When I turned thirty I was pregnant. I called my agent and said, 'I quit.' I did most of my commercial work after that. I was friends with Chuck Blore, who made the first 'Remarkable Mouth' commercial for KIIS radio [in Los Angeles] for me. And the reason he made it for me was because I stuttered. I have since found my voice and don't stutter anymore.

"But I couldn't talk on camera."

Shark's first lips spot was 1970. "Chuck came up with a way to put me on camera where I didn't have to use my words," she said. The camera zoomed in on Shark's lips and then slowly pulled back to reveal her full face. KIIS also put Shark's face on a highway billboard, marking the first time a billboard was used for a single face. She did spots for KSLQ in St. Louis, WNDE in Indianapolis, and a spot in San Diego with baseball's hit king Pete Rose. "Chuck is still out there doing spots. He came up with the concept of 'Remarkable Mouth' and has done them with people all over the country."

WLUP General Manager Les Elias knew of the Los Angeles commercials and hired Lorelei in 1979 for the WLUP-FM television spots. Chicago rock history was sealed with a kiss.

And Shark was not a fan of disco music.

"I only listened to rock 'n' roll," she said. "Are you kidding me? I'm a sixties person. All of the stations I worked for were rock stations. There was one country station. I like Dylan, Beatles, simple. I wasn't a heavy metal rocker. Jefferson Airplane. They briefed me on Disco Demolition. I knew it was a PR stunt. Les [Elias] was a brilliant marketing person. People don't know I produced a couple of comic books for The Loop. They were promotional items called *LOOPS*. People got them for ninety-eight cents each. We hired a talented cartoonist who had worked for Disney, Thom Enriquez. He drew caricatures of The Loop DJs and myself. We did two of them. The stories were based on events of the day, like 'Ronald Ray-Gun' versus 'Jiminy Carter.' I was in on the production of some things.

"Personally, I didn't care about killing disco. I thought the concept was fun."

The cover of the July 1980 issue of *LOOPS* features Dahl, Meier, and other WLUP personalities hoisting a black "Loop" flag in a gallant, Battle of Iwo Jima setting. The cover story—"Steve Dahl and Gary [sic.] Meier vs. Discoman." In panel six on page one, Dahl is depicted stomping out Donna Summer records with his pants sagging low. Seconds later, the crowd at the live "Loop Breakfast Club" remote is chanting: "We Want Lorelei! We Want Lorelei!"

Then WLUP general sales manager Jeff Schwartz said, "As strong as our station was, we really took off after the Lorelei campaign. Let's put it this way: she made the Loop T-shirt very want-able. She was our Farrah Fawcett to our Charlie's Angels. She was our exploding scoreboard. People put a face and a figure to a great radio station."

Shark said, "Between The Loop and *Rocky Horror Picture Show*, I've made a pretty big mark in rock 'n' roll history. And I am a rocker—as it should be."

Shark posed mostly clothed for Playboy magazine and appeared on the *Playboy After Dark* television show. She snagged the gig after attending an open casting call for *Playboy After Dark*. "They asked me if I could dance and I said, 'Yeah, I've danced my entire life,'" Shark said. "I got hired; *Playboy after Dark* was my first job. I was in tons of issues of *Playboy*, mostly in 'The Man Who Reads Playboy,' men's clothing ads. Never ever took my clothes off. That is my claim to fame.

"I didn't mind disco, but I never went to discos. I was a go-go dancer. I did rock 'n' roll. Like on Sunset Strip. I went to the Whiskey A-Go-Go but I didn't dance in a cage. I lived on Sunset during the day. And it was a great day. I'm grateful to have lived in a time that doesn't exist anymore."

Disco Demolition was planned as just another public appearance for "Lorelei." She recalled, "They put me up at the Ritz-Carlton. I did the gig the next day and was supposed to come home right after the game. I went to the event in a black skirt and The Loop shirt. I didn't know what to wear. Before the event I was in a penthouse in downtown Chicago. It was a party for people who owned the station. I had to go from a cocktail party with executives to being on the field. I signed my posters before the event. I didn't have much to do with any planning. I was picked up and taken around: 'Now you're here, now you're there, now you're doing this, now you're doing that.'

"I am living a great life these days. I have a nice place in Beverly Hills where I can walk to parks and shopping, but I spend most of my time in Malibu. I have a lovely place on the ocean. It feels like I'm on a ship. Life has treated me very well."

Steve Dahl and Lorelei Shark with Mike Veeck

14. HOW DISCO DEMOLITION WAS DESIGNED

Just like a disco dance floor, the promotional event was the result of many loose, moving parts . . .

Tom Graye was the star disco DJ on WDAI. Ever the provocateur, Dahl would encourage listeners to throw marshmallows at Graye whenever he made a public appearance.

"Then I recorded 'Do Ya Think I'm Disco,'" Dahl said of his spoof of Rod Stewart's "Do Ya' Think I'm Sexy." He continued, "I went to a bar in Hanover Park with Teenage Radiation where it was packed. There was a mini-riot in the parking lot. We had a gig [on June 2, 1979] at the Pointe East in [the south suburb of] Lynwood, which was this big rock club with a disco upstairs. That got shut down by the police, who showed up in riot gear. It wasn't really that well covered. That was bizarre. I was happy just playing clubs and making a few hundred bucks. I didn't have any sense it was growing. I was just trying to make money on the side."

Roman J. Sawczak grew up in the Roseland area and moved to the south suburb of Lansing in 1972. He was guitarist in a band called Cartune that played Boston and Foreigner covers. Cartune met Dahl at the Pointe East on June 2, the day of the show. "It is the lost event," he said. "Everyone knows about Disco Demolition but this was the whole set up." Formerly the Poison Apple, Pointe East was a disco that had begun to feature live rock 'n' roll one night a month. "Rock was a big deal for them," Sawczak said. "[Cartune] happened to play there right before the disco takeover. I don't think any of us were listeners at the time. We knew of Steve. We informed him we had learned the song ["Do Ya' Think I'm Disco"] in case he wanted to try it live and he went for it."

When Cartune left the early afternoon sound check with Dahl, they found more than one hundred people lined up in the parking lot. "When the club was packed, it could hold over 1,000 people, but over 2,000 people showed up. It wasn't good when they ran out of beer before we even took the stage. Steve had a couple disco dancers come out and dance on stage. It was the biggest mistake. People started heaving beer cups at them. We had to get the dancers off the stage. It was so quick when the cops shut the place down. It was before ten o'clock. They lined both sides of the exits with cops with riot helmets and batons making a path for people."

WLUP promotion director Dave Logan was at the June 2 Pointe East concert, when Donna Summer's "Hot Stuff" was the number one hit in America. "Someone stupidly threw a bottle at the cops," Logan said. "A skirmish. As I was getting ready to go to bed there was the late night news on WGN-TV with Marty McNeely. There was a red flag with a black fist holding a rifle and the word 'RIOT' was on the graphic. They opened up with, 'Radio station promotion gets a little out of hand.' Monday morning I come in to the station and say, 'We were on the news last night, but nothing was as bad as it sounded.' Of course we started to realize Steve at the clubs could be very successful for us. The Monday after we have our regular meeting in promotion, sales, and programming. Jeff Schwartz walks in and says, 'The White Sox need a promotion, in order to get this [advertising] buy.' That's how every meeting opened up with Jeff. We did it with Budweiser, Chevy dealers. Every major advertiser is coming in looking for a promotion.

"We made millions at The Loop with cruises, Johnny [Brandmeier's] concerts, Danny [Bondacue's] boxing matches. It hadn't really happened with Steve and Garry. I said, 'We're getting real traction with this disco thing, Steve and Garry's appearances. What would you think about doing one of these with the White Sox?'"

Dahl said, "Jeff Schwartz and Mike Veeck must have been talking about it. I didn't really have a relationship with Mike. I maybe met him once or twice that night and one time after that? I don't know who was on the front line of the idea. I do know Bill Veeck broke bad on me after, and so I broke bad on them. It's between Jeff, Dave Logan, and Mike—how it all happened, based on other stuff I was doing. They asked me to do it and I said, 'I don't know if that's a good idea. The Sox game was originally Teen Night, but they weren't drawing. I didn't really want to do it. What was the attendance? Five thousand? Even if I tripled that it would only be half full. I reluctantly did it thinking the whole time it was going to be a failure. Even if I drew 5,000 people, that would be a lot of people to draw for a radio person. But it would still look empty and stupid. I have to stand up there and blow up records in front of 5,000 people."

Schwartz said, "Dahl drove me crazy for two and a half months before the event, because in his mind, success would still look like failure. If we draw 10,000 people, the park still looks empty. Up until the day of, he was, 'Goddamnit, I hate doing this. This is going to be nothing.' So I'm going crazy because he's driving me crazy."

Dahl also recruited his new friends Cartune to record his rendition of "Do Ya' Think I'm Sexy." They rehearsed in Bolingbrook and recorded the first sessions at Tanglewood Studios in Brookfield. Sawczak recalled, "Jim Peterik was involved with Tanglewood. We recorded 'Skylab,' 'Hump Day Fever' and 'Do Ya' Think I'm Disco.' Then we re-recorded 'Do Ya' Think I'm Disco' in Evanston for Ovation Records."

Mitch Michaels recalled the WLUP staff meeting about Disco Demolition a few days before the event, and just six

Steve Dahl

weeks after the Pointe East appearance. He said the meeting included Schwartz, station manager Les Elias, program director Jesse Bullett, and Mike Veeck. Schwartz did not recall the staff meeting, but he said that doesn't mean that it did happen. "I'm not big on staff meetings," he said. "And don't forget—everybody was at Disco Demolition," said Mitch Michaels. "Today everyone who said they were there claims we had 200,000 people."

Michaels said, "We all wrote an attendance number on a blackboard. The point was to put fans in the seats because the Sox sucked. Even when they win they don't draw anybody. I think the highest number on the board was 28,000. To Mike's defense, I think he looked at that number and said, 'Okay, this is the kind of security I need.' He didn't have an Andy Frain down every aisle. And kids wound up going down the aisles and climbing over the seats."

Veeck knew the ins and outs of security. In 1975, he booked the Bay City Rollers to perform in between games of a double-header at Comiskey Park. The boy band was riding high on the fumes of its hit "S-A-T-U-R-D-A-Y Night." WLS-AM personalities Bob Sirott and John "Records" Landecker hosted the mini-concert.

"You never heard this story," Veeck said. "I'm in the center field bleachers. I say to the manager of the Bay City Rollers, 'Here is the deal. We have 4,000 fourteen-year-old girls. The only people security can't handle are fourteen-year-old girls. You don't know where to grab them. We had to watch people spread all over the warning track. They would crush these girls. Back in those days, we only had a few women on the security team; it's not what you have today, where you can move a whole melee.'"

Logan pointed out, "In addition to tons of people showing up just because they hated disco, you had families. Mom or Dad could bring their five kids to a double-header for seven bucks [ninety-eight cents each]. It was the greatest bargain in the history of sports, not to mention, for a lot of people, the biggest release they ever had. As the radio station was launching and growing we needed big promotions to blow wind in our sails.

"And it was a strong wind that took us to number one."

Michaels reflected, "I can't imagine Steve (Dahl) was that repulsed by disco. This was a shtick. He got fired for the fucking format change (at WDAI). That would piss me off and make me anti-disco. And the shtick was perfect and he certainly played it well."

Lorelei Shark and Steve Dahl autograph posters

Disco records blowing up on the field

15. HOW DISCO DEMOLITION WENT DOWN

*L*ike many good rock 'n' roll parties, Disco Demolition involved fancy hotels and expensive drinks.

"They had an afternoon cocktail party for the advertisers at the Ritz-Carlton before the event," Dahl said. "I had to dress up in that fucking army uniform. We got to the ballpark with Lorelei and Garry Meier. We were signing posters. There were several hundred people. I wasn't even getting paid."

In a separate interview, Meier said, "We talked about it on the air that morning, obviously: 'Come out if you want to be a part of this.' After our show—I remember it vividly—the station had a reception for advertisers at the Ritz-Carlton. We had lunch and several hours later we were going to the ballpark with these clients. It was all pretty calm. When we pulled up to Comiskey Park, we started to feel this was going to be a little crazier than we could imagine. There were so many people outside the park who couldn't get tickets. We got out and went into the gravel parking lot on the east side. We hung out as fans came up and talked to us. We did that for about a half hour before we went into the park. We made our way to the press box and you could see the place filling up. You could feel the vibe was pretty strong."

Cheap Trick's Rick Nielsen was at the event, at least at the beginning. "I just wanted to see what was going on," he said. "[But] it didn't look like my kind of party. I went to the Hyatt by McCormick Place. I went to check in and Joe Walsh came to the front desk. He said, 'Rick! Let's get in *Rolling Stone*.' He had an electric chainsaw. He wanted to start at the front desk. I said, 'I'll meet you up in your room.' Back then, he carried an electric chainsaw with him. We've been friends ever since."

Back at Comiskey, Dahl and company were ensconced in the Bard's Room, the private upper deck restaurant for owners and members of the media. "We had a free dinner and got drunk," Dahl said. "But I sobered up pretty quickly when I hit that field."

On the field, White Sox manager Don Kessinger was featured in a pre-game Special Olympics award presentation. White Sox coach Joe Sparks ran a Special Olympics clinic that concluded around five p.m. Alan Cassman sang the National Anthem around 5:30.

"[Lorelei] had stage fright," Veeck said. "She stuttered. We could barely get her on field and we paid her the princessly sum of 350 or 500 dollars. She was scared to death."

On the spur of the moment Lorelei was recruited to throw out the first pitch of the ill-fated double-header.

She was not a baseball fan. She did not live in Chicago. In her entire thirty-two years, she had attended one Los Angeles Dodgers game. "All of a sudden they said, 'You're throwing out the ball,'" Shark remembered. "Had I known, I would have practiced. I actually think Steve wanted to and he wasn't happy because I did. The catcher (Mike Colbern, a reserve catcher) came up pretty close to me and they said, 'Okay, throw it' and I tried my best."

Dahl said, "I was standing there dressed in that fucking army helmet and suit and holding a first pitch baseball with no one to throw it to. I wish I had the presence of mind to hold on to that baseball."

Chicago sportscaster Les Grobstein would go on to work with Dahl and Meier, WSCR (AM-670) and WMVP (AM-1000) among others. But on the day of Disco Demolition, "The Grobber," as Dahl nicknamed him, was broadcasting Chicago Hustle games on WCBR-FM (92.7, The Bear). Grobstein said he left the woman's pro basketball summer league game to get to Comiskey Park.

"I remember people in the left field upper deck pouring lighter fluid down the left field foul pole—which was metallic so it wasn't going to burn," Grobstein said.

The Detroit Tigers beat the White Sox 4-1 in the first game which was played in a snappy two hours and thirty-eight minutes. Tigers relief pitcher Aurelio Lopez refused to warm up in the bullpen for the first game because fans were already chucking records and firecrackers on the field.

Meier said, "We watched the first game from the press box. Every now and then you'd see an album

Frisbee whiz by and you'd go, 'Well, that's interesting.' Then we had to make our way down to the Jeep underneath the stands. We went outside the park to come in through center field."

Longtime Chicago rock 'n' roll photographer Paul Natkin was hired by WLUP-FM to document the evening. The native of West Rogers Park in Chicago would go on to become a Rolling Stones tour photographer in 1989 and 1994, and staff photographer for The Oprah Winfrey Show from 1986 to 1991, but there would never be anything as in-your-face as Disco Demolition.

"Before the game, Greg Gumbel (then of WMAQ-TV) interviewed Steve," said Natkin, a lifelong White Sox fan. "I just started taking pictures of everything. Steve was posing with fans. About the seventh inning they came and got us. We went under the bleachers and they had all the records in this big box. The center field door opened up and we went out towards second base. We were all standing in a circle, a couple camera men. We all just walked out."

A convertible Jeep was parked in center field. The Jeep was supposed to take a slow tour around the warning track and Dahl and Meier were going to wave to the crowd from the back of it.

Dahl said, "When that door opened and I saw all those people . . . And then it was, 'What the fuck?' They are throwing beers and cherry bombs at us. And they're the people that like us!"

Meier recalled, "We went on the warning track around the perimeter of the field and I remember beer raining down on us. We were on the Jeep with Lorelei and she was absolutely frightened. She didn't live in Chicago. She didn't know the build up to this. She was just pulled in for the promotion. As the beer came down I really think she thought we were doomed." Lorelei admitted, "I was pretty frightened, not of the people, but of everyone getting out of control. When we were coming in on the Jeep they were throwing full beers at us. We could have ended up in the hospital. I remember being put on the Jeep with Steve and we drove out of the stadium. I was yelling and having fun. The worst part was I didn't get to come home that night [to Los Angeles] to see my kids. I had to stay over an extra night because we couldn't leave the stadium. We were in the press box. Steve was up there. Mitch [Michaels]. Garry [Meier], and other people from the station. They kept me up there until the entire thing was over, which was hours. They were treating it like it was an attack, which it wasn't. It was just a bunch of kids having fun."

Grobstein recalled, "I bet 75 percent of the people running around the field had no idea who Harry Caray was, who Bill Veeck was, and didn't give a hoot about baseball. They were just there to have fun." Grobstein also worked for Sports Phone, the 976-1313 number where fans called to get up-to-the-minute sports news. Ironically, the Sports Phone offices were on the thirty-first floor of the John Hancock building, then six floors below the Loop. But Grobstein also worked for the Associated Press and the ABC radio network. He was covering the White Sox for AP.

"I called AP and said, 'You wouldn't believe what's happening,'" Grobstein said. "They thought it was a non-story. Eventually they called my pocket pager and they said, 'Yeah, maybe we should do something about this.' I said, 'Yeah, you got a riot here.'"

Melrose Pyrotechnics were in charge of the actual demolition.

The firm had a relationship with the White Sox that dated back to the 1959 American League championship season. Melrose was founded in 1955 in Melrose Park, and is now located outside of La Porte, Indiana, the home turf of baseball maverick Charlie O. Finley. Melrose does the fireworks for Navy Pier, the City of Chicago, the Chicago Bears, Kansas City Royals, Kane County Cougars, and many others.

"We were the first exploding scoreboard, and that's how we got started with the White Sox," firm president Michael Cartolano said. "I remember my father telling the story that Bill Veeck asked what would make a good fireworks show every night. My Dad said, 'If you did 400 dollars every night, it would be a nice fireworks show. So Bill said, 'So let's make it 500 dollars.' That's how the relationship started. My sister company [East Coast Pyrotechnics] still does work for Michael Veeck."

Michael Cartolano was twenty-two years old in 1979. He set off all the home runs at Old Comiskey Park that season and helped set up the Disco Demolition show for his father Anthony.

"When we got to the stadium, there wasn't one garbage dumpster or bin," Cartolano recalled. "There were twenty or thirty of them. They collected an album at every gate. So we chose just to put one wooden box on the field, thank God. We wanted an aerial audible effect, like if someone did a twenty-one-gun salute into the sky. We placed the records strategically around the edge of the box which was eight feet by four feet by six feet, four feet tall. We were careful not to explode the box, we just wanted to make sure the albums came out of the box. It wasn't made to make a huge boom out of it.

"We had a wire coming back into the 'Elephant Gate,' in the center field area where we pushed the button. We had it tied to a handle on the outside of the box. When it was detonated, the end of the box pushed itself open and pulled the wire out of [late part-time Melrose worker] Mike [Delaney's hand] as he pushed the button. It was all done electronically."

Cartolano took a pause and agreed that he had a blast looking back at the event. "It was a crazy, crazy night," he said. "We're a fireworks display company and we never touched anything like this. And we never will again." Melrose's resume includes First Place in the Da Nang International Fireworks Competition in Vietnam (2013) and first place in the L'International des Feux Loto in Quebec, Canada (2006).

The records were blown up, and Dahl and Meier found seats in the Jeep. Like a good war photographer, Paul Natkin did not retreat. He jumped on the hood of the Jeep and continued to fire away. "It was pretty scary," recalled Natkin, who was shooting with Nikon and Hasselblad cameras. "The driver of the Jeep freaked out because people were throwing beers at us, so he just floored it. We went a little ways and then back out the center field door. I'm holding on to the windshield wiper to keep from falling off the hood of the Jeep—the windshield wiper."

During the first game of the scheduled double-header, Mitch Michaels did a couple of play-by-play innings with Harry Caray and former major league outfielder Jimmy Piersall. Michaels attempted to tell Caray why people brought records into the ballpark. "It was a concert atmosphere and not a baseball atmosphere," Michaels said. "Nobody gave a shit if the White Sox won or lost the first game." Dahl recalled Piersall's television commentary: "'These aren't baseball fans; they are fans of far out.'"

White Sox left hander Ken Kravec was scheduled to pitch the second game. The chaos was cresting. "I was in the clubhouse getting ready," Kravec recalled from his home in Sarasota, Florida. "Stretching out, getting some heat. I was oblivious to everything, although I knew they were going to blow up some disco albums. I didn't know how many people were in the stands. By the time I walked out there Steve Dahl had finished his thing. Ron Schueler was the [White Sox] pitching coach, and he and I were walking to the bullpen where I was going to warm up. If you remember, the bullpen was right next to the stands. And the wall was only three feet high. The fans were right there. And the upper deck hung over quite a bit.

"So I began my warm ups, and after five minutes every now and then a shoe would fly by me. Then a couple more shoes. And then they started to Frisbee the albums and I mentioned to Ron, 'I don't think it's a good idea for us to be standing here.' Ron says, 'Let's go out on the main mound.' So we went out on the field to finish up on the main mound. I threw ten pitches, and the next thing you know, the fans stormed the field. No hassles. I grabbed my hat, held onto my glove, and walked off the field. Nobody bothered me. I stood in the dugout for a little while and walked in the clubhouse. I didn't pay much attention to it until they mentioned there was another 10,000, 15,000 people outside the stadium. I do remember looking up into the stands, and it was more than sold out. I couldn't even see the aisles in the upper deck. It was just wall-to-wall people. Obviously when they couldn't get it under control the police from the outside came inside. They had the helmets on."

Steve Trout recalled, "There were many people outside the stadium that couldn't get in. Even without social media it turned out to be a huge crowd. When they started blowing up the albums, I came out of the locker room to the dugout. I was sitting with [outfielder] Ralph Garr and [first baseman] Lamar Johnson. They both had bats in their hands. If one fan jumps on the field, there's five, [then] fifteen, and now the field is taken over. They weren't as rowdy as much as they were just partying and running around. It was anti-disco so it had a feeling of anti-something. So I ask Lamar and Ralph, 'You guys have those bats, are you going to use them against these people?' They were two of my best buddies in baseball. They said, 'If they come down in the dugout we are.'"

Trout told Garr and Johnson the hooligans were just fun-loving south siders having a good time. "There got to be so many people when the mounted police came on the field they made us go in the locker room," he said. "We were the only three in the dugout. Most of the other guys didn't want to be part of it.

"We thought it was just going to be another promotion like, 'Dog Night.' No one expected such a large crowd."

Kravec looked back at the night with a trace of innocence. "Think: back then, there was basically no security," he said. "There was security in the stands to break up fights, but there weren't checkpoints like there are now to walk into a stadium. A couple fans came into the clubhouse. What are the chances of that happening nowadays? Maybe that's when [White Sox manager] Don Kessinger locked the clubhouse door. I know the majority, if not all, the players were in the clubhouse. As it escalated you would peek out there to see what was going on. I went out for a couple minutes a couple times to see what was going on, but I didn't sit in the dugout and watch all the events. Especially once the police came on the field, it was time to seek shelter."

DJ Michaels said, "The place went bonkers after they blew up the records. People started jumping out of the stands. It was like the rats leaving a ship. A few, then more, then total chaos. Dahl was freaked out." Veteran *Chicago Tribune* baseball writer Paul Sullivan was at the game—not on assignment. His father Dan was a White Sox season ticket holder with box seats down the first base line. Dan Sullivan was a salesman for C-E Refractories steel company in East Chicago and Gary, Indiana.

During the steamy summer of 1979, Paul Sullivan was a nineteen-year-old laborer with Koppers, Co., a steel mill in east Chicago. He carried buckets of cement with bricklayers. "I used my dad's tickets that night," Sullivan said over a beer in Bill Veeck's corner at Miller's Pub in downtown Chicago. "I went because of the Steve Dahl thing, but I had gone to a lot of games. It wasn't like I wasn't interested in the baseball, although they did suck that year. I had gone to the Dahl disco thing in June at Pointe East. That was pretty raucous and a lot of fun so I thought, 'This will be good.' Although I didn't think it would be like that."

"I was with my buddies and we brought in some Jack Daniel's to mix with Cokes. The first people I saw were jumping out from left field. We laughed and said, 'That's crazy'. Then it was like popcorn. Everyone started jumping on the field at the same time. We said, 'All right, let's go.' We jumped on top of the dugout. I was very worried my Dad was going to find out I was on the field. People were sliding into the bases. At some point I went into the Tigers dugout. We were messing around with the Jack Daniel's, and Tigers coach Alex Grammas [a former Cub and St. Louis Cardinal] said, 'Is that your bottle?' I said 'Yeah,' and he said, 'Hand it to me, would you son?' I said, 'Yes sir.' I gave him the bottle. He asked me to leave the dugout, so I went

Steve Trout

onto the field. He was very nice about it. I could see [Tigers pitcher] Mark Fidrych peeking out from the end of the Tigers dugout. He was one of my favorite players. I think he was injured. A lot of Tigers were sticking their heads out to to see what was going on, and Grammas was going, 'Get back in here, get back in here' to get in the clubhouse. I left, but before leaving the field I got a piece of turf. I put it my pocket.

"For awhile it looked like it was going to go on forever and I got tired of it. When the cops came we scrammed."

The electronic "Sox-O-Gram" on the center field scoreboard meekly suggested "Please return to your seats." Dahl laughed and said, "Mitch Michaels tried to do a 'Back To Your Seats!' chant. It was funny and weird. No one else was chanting. Bill Veeck came down and talked. Harry Caray thought it was kind of cool. Jimmy Piersall was flipping out."

Mike Veeck recalled, "Harry was a pro. He was the dance band on the Titanic, playing through the disaster. My favorite image is my old man and Harry standing at home plate with the Sox-O-Gram reading 'Please return to your seats.' Like Diana Ross, 'Stop! In the Name of Love.' Harry knew exactly what it was. It was a promotion and it had been unbelievably successful. My old man said it best and no one paid attention, 'It was a promotion that worked too well.' Then my Dad went out and took the public berating for me.

"Piersall, on the other hand, never liked me and I never liked him. He goes, 'These aren't ball fans!' Really? Wow! There was a haze over the top of the ballpark! When did that occur to him? In those days the broadcast was piped through the ballpark and his microphone was on. I went up and strangled him. He was on the air and that was probably not a wise decision. But he was fueling the event, instead of 'That idiot Veeck did this, people should return to their seats,' he was like, 'They're running around like animals! So people were running out of their houses like, 'I gotta get over there.'"

WLUP promotions director Dave Logan was in the press box listening to the Tigers television crew that included beloved Detroit Hall of Famer Al Kaline as color man. "Live on the air, [announcer and former Tiger] George Kell goes, 'I can't believe this is happening to the game of baseball, Al,'" Logan recalled. "And Al says, 'And in America, too, George!' Man, I grew up in Detroit idolizing these guys."

Michaels said, "Mike Veeck came to me and said, get on the P.A. and see if you can get these people off the field. So we did what we would do at a concert—'Back To Your Seats!' Harry Caray was my all time favorite baseball announcer. He had been somewhere, in the Bard's Room, having a few Budweisers. We were making a little progress. People were starting to move out a bit. Then Harry comes up, grabs the microphone and says [impersonating Caray], 'What the *hell* is going on here?' When Harry Caray says, 'Give me the microphone,' you give Harry Caray the microphone. We lost the momentum. Even if we had got everybody off the field I still think they would have forfeited the second game."

Dahl volunteered to go on the P.A. system to tell the crowd to chill.

He was not allowed to assist.

"Steve absolutely would have been able to get people back to their seats," Veeck said. "Certainly him more than my old man, Harry, or Mitch Michaels. I'm sure Harry and Dad didn't let Steve do it. Dad always felt the station knew this was going to happen. But if Steve had done it, a number of people would have returned to their seats, and again it is crowd control. If you see the swallows returning to Capistrano, then you have a shot."

Mike Veeck was on the field for the entire event. He recalled, "Dahl took one round [around the field] and went upstairs in the press box. Nancy Faust was scared to death. I've been through civil rights marches and I didn't look at this and say, 'We're going to have a riot.' It went bad after the explosion and once the fire started I'm thinking, 'This ain't Arthur Brown'." (The Crazy World of Arthur Brown had the 1968 hit "Fire.") "We used our regular fireworks guys [Melrose]. There was a small charge, maybe half a stick of dynamite [underneath the records]. But the actual rockets on the field were low level. If someone turned wrong you would have a problem. Luckily the fans were all stoned. If that had been a baseball crowd of drinkers, then it would have been what people call a 'riot.' History will determine what it was like, but they were 'enthusiastic.'"

Pyrotechnician Cartolano remembered, "They brought in the mounted police to get people off the field and pushed everybody out. The fire wasn't started by the fireworks. The fire was started by the rioters. They tore urinals off the walls."

Trout, Garr, and Johnson watched all the smoke and fire from the dugout. "Oh my goodness," Trout said. "People tore the bases apart. Home plate was gone. There was a big spot in center field where the albums had been blown up. There was vinyl everywhere. I walked out to look at center field and I heard something go by me. It was an album from the upper deck and landed next to my right foot. It was stuck in the ground. I said, 'Holy shit, I could have been killed by the Village People.' It seriously was the Village People. That's what I remember about that night. Along with Eddie Farmer getting into a fight in the parking lot. And he could fight."

Ed Farmer was raised in Evergreen Park. Farmer, born in 1949, attended St. Rita High School on the southwest side where he played baseball and basketball. "We found out early the second game was going to be called," the six-foot-five, 200-pound Farmer recalled during a pre-game interview at U.S. Cellular Field. "I went to the family room and got my wife and my daughter Shanda, who was three. I got them in the car and somebody pounded on the roof of my car. I told my wife, 'Anyone pounds on the roof of my Porsche again I'm going to get out and knock them for a loop.' My daughter goes, 'Daddy, what's a loop?' I said, 'You're about to find out.' I got out and this guy came after me. I took him out pretty good. His buddy jumped on my neck and then rolled on top of this guy's Corvette. This was right out on Shields, Bill Veeck Drive.

"The police came and I shook hands with everybody, but the one guy was not doing too good. I had a crease over my eye, but it wasn't bleeding. I had a mouse from the two guys who were trying to handle me. I was really strong. I wasn't going to take it. I couldn't do anything about the guy around my neck. So I was hammering the guy I had in a chokehold."

The resilient Farmio threw four shut out innings in the first game of the double-header. "I remember records flying by me when I was pitching," he said. "When I was going in after the game someone grabbed my hat. I went in the stands and got it back. I don't think anyone knew how much they used to detonate those records. They flew up at least twenty-five, thirty feet in the air. When they started coming out on the field, Bill Veeck came out. You know, a 'voice of reason'—Bill Veeck. Great guy, but nobody was going to listen to him. The field was torn up. I really felt sorry for Gene Bossard and his son Roger, taking care of the field. Now they had to appease the owner on something that was created by the owner, more or less. People were hanging from the guard wires on the scoreboard in center field. People tried to break down the club house door. There was a four-by-six plank holding the door back and so many people were distressing that plank. They finally got the people off and there was the odor of fire in the ball park.

"It was lunacy defined."

Paul Sullivan leaned forward in the dimly lit Veeck's Corner at Miller's Pub. For a minute, you swore the framed "Baseball Couldn't Shut Him Out" *Sports Illustrated* cover picture of Veeck winked at anyone who was listening. "I loved Bill Veeck," said Paul Sullivan. "I felt bad for him that night, because when he came out to tell people to get off the field, that's when I left. But you could tell no one else respected him enough to listen to him."

Michael Cartolano recalled, "It was so crowded my brother Rocco parked against the wall in the outside parking lot. They actually took one of the police barricades and put it on the roof of his Ford pick-up truck and climbed over the wall using the barricade. It crushed the roof of the cab of his truck."

The Cartolano brothers are rock 'n' roll fans and remain Dahl fans today. "All of our guys liked WLUP, so this was exciting for us," Michael Cartolano said. "Steve had the army fatigues on and the Jeep. It was so cool to see Steve, Garry, and Lorelei."

Anne Sorkin was at Disco Demolition. She went with her friends from Proviso East High School in the western suburb of Maywood. Sorkin comes from a musical family, so naturally she would find her way into the event. Her father is Chicago acoustic musician Dave Prine. Her uncles are Nashville based singer-songwriters Billy Prine and John Prine.

The entire Prine family attended Proviso East. Dave, a retired electrical engineer who still plays banjo, dobro, fiddle, and guitar is the oldest of the brothers. The 1979 event fell during the summer after Sorkin's graduation from Proviso East.

"Disco was not on my Dad's list of anything he would even tolerate listening to," Sorkin said. "A lot of us listened to Steve Dahl. It was unlike anything I ever heard on radio. I loved how he was so real. I loved his characters, like Irma C. Residue. We all hated disco. In my school we were the underdogs, so to speak.

Disco took off overnight. So if you were a rock 'n' roller you felt marginalized."

In mid-July 1979, Sorkin was staying with her grandmother Verna Valentine Prine on 14th Avenue in Melrose Park. Her parents were away on vacation with her sister Jean. Sorkin was eager to get to the game for the ninety-eight cent admission charge along with a slab of disco vinyl. "Of course, none of us had disco records," Sorkin said. "But my sister had Donna Summer. She's four years younger than I am and she was kind of the rebel. Whatever I did, she was going to do something different. She was going into high school and that was going to be her thing. So I went to my parent's house and raided

Anne Sorkin

my sister's collection. I took enough records to pass out to my friends. And we had some extras in the car. None of us were baseball fans, but we wanted to see Steve."

The anti-disco posse crowded into a Dodge Dart to drive from Maywood to Comiskey Park. "When we got there we didn't expect it to be so mobbed," Sorkin recalled. "We walked right in after a gate had been broken. There was already smoke on the field. You could sit anywhere. My friends starting throwing the disco records like Frisbees. A lot of my friends ran the bases. I walked around the field. The news characterized it as a bunch of 'hoodlums' and 'law breakers.' I never felt that it wasn't safe.

"It was just a bunch of people having fun."

Once the second game was cancelled, the group retreated to the Ground Round restaurant on North Avenue in Melrose Park.

"My grandmother saw it on the news and was worried about me," said Sorkin. who teaches special needs students at Betsy Ross School in Forest Park. "There were no cell phones of course, so I called her from the Ground Round to let her know I was okay. She said, 'Okay, have fun.' But when my mom and dad returned from vacation and found out she let me go to this, they were pretty mad. But it was harmless. The media played it up like we were a bunch of delinquents."

John Iltis was the publicist for WLUP.

"We'd been working with WLUP for a couple years doing all sorts of promotions," said Iltis, who began his Chicago PR career in 1965. "We did the public appearances at various bars with the Loop girls. We represented King Richard's Faire and had them at Comiskey a couple of times. It was easy. You called up Mike Veeck and it was, 'Bring 'em in. We have a spare night on Thursday.' They told me what they were going to do [with "Teen Night"] and I said, 'Oh, shit, what are you talking about? A dollar for each person to get in and they have to bring a record? Do you know where those records are going? All over the place, I knew it was going to go down as something unique."

Iltis was in the Comiskey press box when things went south. He was on the phone with local television stations assuring them there was not a riot at Comiskey Park. "I was trying to do my job," he said in gallant tones. "I had friends at the stations. They said, 'Iltis, get a grip. It is a riot. They're climbing outside into the stadium.' There was damage control but there was nothing I could do. The TV cameras were there and recording everything, people pulling up sod off the infield."

Chicago mayor Jane Byrne was having dinner that night with her husband, former Chicago newspaperman Jay McMullen. They heard about the commotion and stopped by Comiskey Park. Byrne, after all, moved into the Cabrini-Green housing projects in 1981. Mayor Byrne shook hands with the rock 'n' roll fans from the safety of her car. A reporter asked her if she was pro- or anti-disco. She answered, "Oh, don't try to get me involved in that!"

Chicago artist-author-raconteur Tony Fitzpatrick trekked into Disco Demolition from his home in the western suburb of Lombard. He was looking for some kind of light.

"What I remember is being so lost," said Fitzpatrick who appeared on WLUP in various roles between 1987 and 1996. "I was nineteen years old and I knew I wanted to be an artist. But I had a job cement finishing and making miniature caskets at American Wilbert Vault in Forest Park. My father worked for American Wilbert Vault. I was kind of a Dahl listener. I didn't hate disco, I just didn't care. I thought Nile Rodgers was a fucking monster. When Thelma Houston covered 'Don't Leave Me This Way,' that was hair raising. To me, it was R&B. I brought my sister's Bee Gees record to the game.

"I did understand what Dahl did not like about disco, culturally. I noticed the guys I went to high school with had slid into this bill of goods where they were going to four years of college and take accounting or business, wear a three-piece suit and cease to matter. They were going to go home, sit in front of their TV every night, and bitch at the news. I hated the cultural trappings of disco. I thought, 'I'm not going to be that guy'. It was about the time I knew I was going to be a serious artist and not let anything stand in my way.

"In an odd way, Disco Demolition helped enact my first act," Fitzpatrick said in his studio, his "First Radiant Seabird" painting hanging on a wall behind him. "Disco Demolition set us free. When I jumped on the outfield there was this moment of liberation where I thought, 'I don't have to be like everyone else'. And you know what? By the time there were a few hundred people running around out there, they all had the same fucking goofy grin on their faces. It was like, 'It's okay for a long haired kid who likes rock 'n' roll to be free and stupid.'"

M.C. Antil was working in the White Sox group sales department in 1979. He was assigned to work the field and the gates during Disco Demolition. "The nylon batting cages were sort of melting down. Bill Veeck was on the field and it was so wet from bad drainage and concerts, Bill's peg leg kept sinking into the mud. The poor guy was literally trying to balance on one leg. Harry Caray is yelling for people to get back to their seats. And then the center field gates roll open, and two-by-two on horseback is Chicago's finest, with billy clubs. I guarantee you these are some of the same cops who were in Grant Park in 1968. The fans parted like the red sea when those guys came in.

"There was no real access to get out of the ballpark. We had one a one-way gate, which is now on Bill Veeck Way. When the second game was going to get cancelled we couldn't open the doors to let people out because more people would get in. I was assigned that gate. People were shoving, and there was a sea of humanity. I stood on one of the turnstiles to coach people through. I'm two feet taller than everyone else. And [then I saw former New York Knicks center and head coach] Willis Reed. I was about to say something and he gave me that look, 'If you say something, I'm going to kill you.'

Loop general sales manager Schwartz was hanging around second base during the melee. "Jerry Mickelson [of Jam] saved me from being hurt," he said. "All of a sudden I get pushed on the ground. An album was coming right towards my head. Jerry pushed me down. That's when they hustled us off the field. It was obviously not a baseball crowd."

Natkin remarked, "It showed the power of radio in 1979."

Schwartz said, "I never saw Dahl the rest of the night. Les Elias and I were in Bill Veeck's office at two o'clock in the morning waiting to see what the damage results were from the insurance company, because we were going to pay it. Bill Veeck goes, 'Gentleman, I hope you don't mind. It is real late and my leg is killing me.' And in front of us, he unscrews his leg, puts it on the side of his desk and continues to use it as an ash tray. He says, 'I don't know who [Dahl] is, but boy does he know how to draw people.' Bill was an entrepreneur. He got it.

"We were a hired circus act."

Janet Dahl recalled, "I went to Disco Demolition. I just watched until somebody got me. I don't remember much but I remember seeing Bill Veeck a bit introspective. He didn't seem angry or anxious, just very quiet. My brother Paul was watching the game at a bar in Detroit. He goes, 'Oh my God, that is Steve. That is my brother-in-law!' He couldn't believe it. The next day people were calling me going, 'Are you okay? Were you in the middle of that?' We were fine. And Steve was fine. I thought, 'This is cool. Steve is really popular.' Then there was blowback and people saying mean things, but I was naive then."

Steve Dahl said, "After it was over I sobered up. We stayed [at Comiskey] for a while and I got lectured. Tom Hoyt told me not to bring it up. The station was owned by a U.S. Congressman from Hawaii [Cecil Heftel] and Tom was like, 'Whatever you do, be *cool* about it tomorrow.' I go, 'What does that mean?' He said, 'Don't talk about this.' How could I not talk about it?"

Meier said, "Our boss Tom Hoyt, who was from Texas, leaned into us, 'Whatever you do, be cool on the air tomorrow. Be cool tomorrow.' Why would we not talk about it? It's a huge deal. Police were trying to quell the 'riot.' I wouldn't have classified it a garden variety 'riot,' where people are carrying TV sets and luxury items out of a store. It was teenage angst running itself out. This was our fan base. That's what we attracted and that was fine. They ran around, they pulled up some sod. To be honest I think they could have played that second game."

Dahl said, "Around midnight, Janet, myself, Garry, and my friend Hugh [Surratt, a record promotions guy] went to the Holiday Inn on McClurg Court and just stayed in the room and listened about it on radio. Eddie Schwartz was on all night [on WIND-AM] demanding that I be fired. It was crazy."

Michaels agreed WLUP's political spin only amped up the controversy. "A Republican congressman from Hawaii and you've got people blowing up disco records in Chicago," Michaels said. "And it is your radio station, I guess that would bother you."

Grobstein recalled, "The White Sox PR people put out an announcement that the game was postponed. [Tigers manager] Sparky Anderson said, 'Postponed, my ass. This has to be a forfeiture.' It was left in the hands of the American League. The next morning nobody knew what was happening. There was no internet, no cell phones. I got in touch with one of the PR people at the American League before they put an announcement out. She said, 'Based on what happened, this game is forfeited and should not be rescheduled.' I beat all the newspapers and electronic media. Newspapers hated radio and TV people anyway. The White Sox were furious, but there was nothing they could do. Detroit won 9-0."

Dahl has vivid memories of television crews waiting for his arrival the next morning when he showed up for work on the thirty-seventh floor of the John Hancock building.

"It was on the front page of the newspapers," he said. "How could I not talk about this? Janet and I got married, I lost my job. I got this job. It was like the last job in Chicago. I couldn't blow this. So for the first thirty seconds on the air I tried not to talk about it. Then, it was fuck it, and I went on with it. Different sponsors pulled out but at the same time they realized the folly of not talking about it."

Michaels took a deep breath and said, "The [publicity] we got out of this thing? The station was already really hot. It literally was the single greatest radio promotion in the history of the business. Okay, there were arrests and some damage, but it wasn't a catastrophic event where people ended up in bad places. This really gave us a gauge of the power of our radio station. I have never seen anything like it [since]. We went on the air on March 19, 1979 and beat WLS two books straight up. The second book came out in September [two months after the event]. WLUP got a huge bounce and the station never came close to ratings like that again.

"It really was magical."

Management softened when national press started calling Disco Demolition the most successful radio promotion of all time. "Then they got into it," Dahl said. "I had to weigh, 'Do I do what they say, keep my job, and lose my credibility, or do I retain my credibility and maybe lose my job?' I decided to go with credibility, which worked out for me. It was a big turning point for me. It was unfair for me not to talk about it, but part of it was that a U.S. Congressman owned the station. He only owned eight stations, something like that, so I don't think he wanted the heat. Honestly, the station promoted it and somebody must have made money off it. But it wasn't me. There were people who had the presence of mind to have bootleg T-shirts made up that they were selling. But I was caught unaware. I didn't think I was that popular. I hadn't had good ratings until that point. I started in March [of 1979] at The Loop. My first quarterly ratings would have come out at the time of Disco Demolition. There was no indicator that [Meier and I] were popular. And then almost every big market radio station copied that. They had an 'Anti-Disco Army' and things. There was a lot of copycat disco bashing too. It's not like I franchised it. God knows what else other people did in the name of it. I know in Detroit at WRIF Jim Johnson and George Baier [called "Dick The Bruiser"] had an anti-disco army [called "D.R.E.A.D"—Detroit Rockers Engaged In The Abolition of Disco] and membership cards. A lot of those people weren't as talented as we were, so who knows what they said?"

Several WLUP advertisers pulled the plug on the station in the aftermath of Disco Demolition. "Advertisers cancelling was probably stupid because it was proof you actually had access to a lot of people," Dahl reasoned. "Really until 1995, '96 was the first time I heard anything real negative about it. Other than [AM talk show giants] Wally Phillips and Eddie Schwartz, [newspaper columnist] Kup and the regulars being pissed off about it just because it was anarchy. Nothing more than the old guard hating the up and coming people. I actually never put that much thought into any of it. I've been forced to reconstruct it and have some kind of purpose for it."

Steve Dahl autographs a baseball

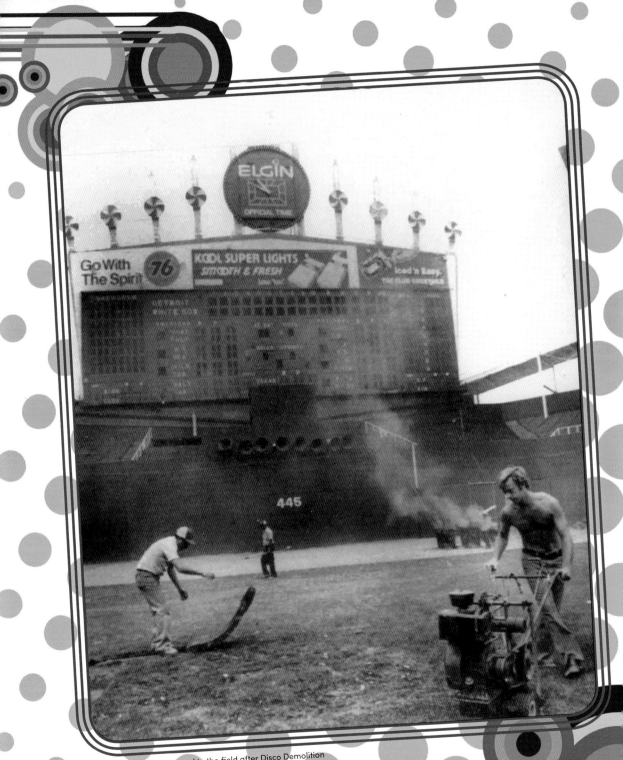

Groundskeepers tend to the field after Disco Demolition

16. LEGENDARY GROUNDS- KEEPER ROGER BOSSARD: THE MORNING AFTER

Roger Bossard was the only subject in this book who did not smile while recalling Disco Demolition.

The late 1960s were a turbulent time of liberation, loud rock music, and anti-war demonstrations. While others were smoking grass, Chicago White Sox groundskeeper Roger Bossard elected to join the U.S. Navy in 1967.

Bossard, only eighteen, was shipped to DaNang, Vietnam, where he became a Third Class Machinist Mate. Bossard had already been on the job for two years as an assistant groundskeeper to his father, Gene Bossard.

When people say Roger Bossard is a no-nonsense gentleman, you better believe them. He has earned his stripes. And when Roger Bossard says Disco Demolition was one of his worst days in baseball, you listen.

"As you go through life, there's always the good and bad things you remember," Bossard said early one summer morning in his U.S. Cellular Field office before a 2015 game. "The birth of your children and stuff like that. One of the bad things was Disco Demolition.

"As far as drawing people to an event, it went really well," said Bossard, who returned to his groundskeeping job from the war in 1969. "But when you're a groundskeeper, see a bonfire in center field and the kids running out . . . "

Bossard's spacious office is across the street from the site of Comiskey Park. He almost doesn't want to look in that direction.

"It got scary," Bossard continued. "The ballplayers actually locked themselves in the clubhouse. When the kids started coming down the foul pole, Dad said, 'Make sure they don't take the bases.' So I ran to second and he ran to third. When it got scary, he ran off. If I see my Dad running off, I run off too. So we locked ourselves in the office for a little while. People can say what they want. My job was affected."

Bossard nodded towards a northern wall of more tranquil baseball memories. His miniature 1959 White Sox uniform is framed, from the time he ran around the bases with the kids of beloved White Sox pitcher Billy Pierce. One photo is of Comiskey Park on the day after Disco Demolition.

"There's me the next morning," Bossard said, staring at the picture. "No one has ever seen that picture. If anybody tells you it wasn't that bad or it was funny, I hope you understand where I'm coming from. It's like if I go to your house, and how about if I just take all your furniture and throw it down?"

In the historic picture, the clock in center field says 10:50. While Steve Dahl and Garry Meier were getting mobbed by media on the morning after the event, a shirtless Bossard was alone near second base pushing a side cutter, resodding the field. Another groundskeeper is standing alone in center field like a zombie in a George Romero movie. Clouds of smoke permeate the field, from a fire burning the wooden chairs uprooted from the stands.

"We had the picnic area in left field," Bossard said. "They took out those seats, put them in center field, and lit a bonfire. The grass caught on fire. The picture is the remnants of it. It turned out to be one of the biggest disasters in Major League Baseball history. Mike [Veeck] said it ruined part of his career. It didn't ruin my career, but it certainly affected it for awhile, because when every visiting ballplayer comes in, the first thing he says is, 'God, look at your field.' It took the rest of the season to get it right. We had so many concerts afterwards, this was just part of what was going on. It wasn't a joke to the groundkeepers. This isn't just people just talking to you, now. This is the real deal."

"Around one o' clock in the morning [after the event], Dad called the sod grower," Bossard continued. "He thought Dad was in a bar, 'What, are you joking? You need 700 yards of sod tomorrow?' Dad and I stayed all night at the ballpark. We had a game the next day."

It would be Friday, July 13. Bossard recalled, "We finally left about four in the morning, went home for two hours, and came back because we had to re-sod. I lived in Lansing and Dad lived in South Holland. I've been here over forty-five years and I'm the most fortunate person in the world. I'm doing what I want to do and I've done it my whole life.

"That was the one time I told my Dad I questioned if I was in the right business."

Bossard is a third-generation Major League groundskeeper (although he calls himself a "groundkeeper"). In 1984 and '85, he designed and built the first natural turf soccer fields in Saudi Arabia for the Royal Family, where he had two jumbo jets shipped in carrying refrigerated sod. He builds his irrigation systems around a timer. His keen and focused demeanor is why Paul Sullivan nicknamed Bossard "The Sodfather."

Between 1936 and 1961 Bossard's grandfather Emil was groundskeeper at League Park and Cleveland Municipal Stadium in Cleveland, Ohio. In 1950, Gene Bossard became the youngest groundskeeper in the major leagues when he joined the White Sox at the age of twenty-three. Gene and Bill Veeck worked together during the 1959 "Go Go White Sox" American League championship season.

When Gene retired during the 1983 "Winning Ugly" season, he bequeathed his job to his son. Roger had studied agronomy at Purdue University but bypassed his degree when the White Sox offered him the job. Gene died in 1998 at the age of eighty.

Roger Bossard was thirty in 1979, and he loved disco.

"I remember going downtown and dancing at Faces. Those were the good times."

Technically, some of the Disco Demolition dance floor lives on at U.S. Cellular Field. "The most important part of the field is the infield dirt," Bossard explained. "I took that over here. It was that important. My Dad had it since the 1950s."

Not long after Comiskey was renamed U.S. Cellular Field in 1991, Bossard took a call from a woman in her mid-fifties. She asked if it was true that he imported the infield dirt. "She started crying and I didn't understand," Bossard said. "She said, 'Years ago your father allowed us to put my Dad's ashes on the dirt. So I still know where my Dad is at.' I felt real good about that. To this day we allow ashes on the warning track. I do not allow it on the infield or the grass."

Bossard cannot confirm or deny a story that White Sox shortstop Harry Chappas tried to help clean up the beloved Comiskey Park before the second game forfeit. Comiskey Park pyrotechnicians Anthony Cartolano, his son Michael, and their crew did provide assistance.

"You know when you catch the fish and it's this big?" Bossard said, holding his hands apart. "It's odd how thirty years later it was a shark. I was fighting it for five hours. Maybe Harry [Chappas] went out there, I don't know. But it's a day I'll never forget. The person I felt sorry more than anybody was Bill [Veeck]. Bill was sick. He wasn't feeling well. He had to come down and the kids were mobbing him. They just couldn't get people off the field. The players weren't happy. It wasn't good and obviously it made the organization not look good. But Bill Veeck stood up for his son.

"That's what a father is supposed to do."

Steve Dahl addressees the crowd

Garry Meier and Steve Dahl on the field

17. DISCO DEMOLITION VENDORS SERVE MEMORIES

Baseball players come and go and musical trends ebb and flow, but veteran Chicago baseball vendors have seen it all.

The eternity of baseball season is shadowed by the fleeting promise of a Chicago summer. Few people around a ballpark have the consistent visibility of a vendor. Chicago fans connect with baseball vendors unlike any other sport. The vendor is always ready with a helping hand and a sympathetic beer. And a handful of vendors who worked Disco Demolition can still be found in Chicago.

Robert "Bob" Chicoine is a native of the South Side, Auburn Gresham neighborhood of Chicago. A White Sox fan, he no longer works at U.S. Cellular Field, but can be found selling beer at Wrigley Field and Soldier Field. Chicoine was born in 1951 and has been a ballpark vendor since 1977.

"Chico," as his friends call him, was selling twelve-ounce cans of Schlitz and Stroh's beer in the left field upper deck on the night of Disco Demolition. "The minute we got in, we knew what we were facing," Chicoine said in a conversation over a Chicago-style hot dog (celery salt, sport peppers, poppy seed bun, tomatoes cut like wagon wheels) at Morrie O'Malley's in the western shadow of U.S. Cellular Field. "Some vendors had gone to the [anti-disco] rock club thing Steve Dahl had done in Lynwood, [Illinois]. I was living on the North Side. Some days I drove to Comiskey, but since the vendors told me it was going to be wild, I took the El. The minute I got off the El I could see what was going to happen. This was at least an hour before the first game started."

Chicoine went to to obtain his "item card" which tells the vendor what they are selling and where they are selling it. "The steward was a very cool guy, he could have played in

The Million Dollar Quartet, he had that look," Chicoine recalled. "He told everyone, 'You sell to a minor today, I can't help you.' The drinking age back then was nineteen [for beer]. I'd say a good third of the crowd was under nineteen.

"That first game we were just flooded. We'd come out with two cases at a time, sometimes three, and just set up. You were like a defender of the Alamo. You'd just try to protect your space. I didn't have many problems, outside of a couple grabbers who didn't get anything. Beer was right around ninety cents. We were on the rhythm method. You were supposed to work three games on Schlitz and one on Stroh's. I forgot what I had that night but it didn't matter. People were just buying. No one was watching the game. They cut beer off at some point, maybe a half hour after everyone got on the field. It needed to be done. But I'd say the crowd was more stoned than drunk."

Dave Gaborek was selling soda pop along the lower deck, third base section on the night of Disco Demolition. He retired from vending in 2011 to operate his souvenir shop, Let's Tailgate, at Northwestern University with Cindy Fosco, another former vendor. Fosco was one of the first female vendors to work Soldier Field, but she did not work Disco Demolition.

"I was twenty years old," Gaborek said as he sipped his drink across from Chicoine on the O'Malley's patio. "Of course, this was before social media, and every kid got a smoke signal to come to Comiskey because of Steve Dahl and The Loop. The first game was uneventful, other than a few records flying around. They used to do Beer Case Stacking Day, which they don't do anymore, and let people on the field in an organized fashion. In between the twi-nighter a couple kids jumped on the field. I remember like it was yesterday, one long haired kid jumped out of left field, ran across the outfield, slid into second base, picked up the bag and waved it. That's what started it."

"He grew up to become Ira Glass," Chicoine added.

Gaborek continued, "Kids were climbing foul poles. I saw Andy Frain [an usher] get punched in the face. That's when they wore those white hats and suits. I saw a kid marching from third base to home plate with a marijuana leaf sign. I saw nuns starting to go crazy."

The vendors were canaries in the coal mine that was Comiskey. The ballpark's dark corners lent themselves well to shenanigans, before and after Disco Demolition. Smoking was permitted everywhere. "They had cigarette machines," Gaborek said. "There was a lot of marijuana smoking." Chicoine added, "Under Veeck, the White Sox tolerated a lot of wild behavior. It was routine on a Friday and Saturday night to see two paddy wagons waiting on 35th Street. And on most days they would use both of those, even in crowds of 25,000. There were that many fights. The whole Mack's Truck parking lot [on 33rd Street] was full of buses, many of which were from bars.

The baseball drinking landscape has changed dramatically since 1979. Chicoine reflected, "It is all different, from the pricing point to the kind of person that goes to games, to the fact that it is no longer cool to be drunk in public. I'm sure in that first game [of Disco Demolition] we were up to twenty-some cases of beer [sold]. They were twelve ounces, compared to sixteen ounces today. We got eighteen cents a beer. Now it is down to about ten cents a beer. We could almost count on ten cases for a Sox or Cubs game in the summer of 1979."

Gaborek grew up a White Sox fan in the North Side neighborhood of Logan Square. From 1940 to 1969, his father owned the Duck-Mill Liquors tavern, named after his father Frank (nicknamed 'Duck') and mother Mildred. The tavern was at the corner of Diversey and Hamlin. Duck and Mill gave away White Sox tickets. "He sold Meister Brau and Falstaff and they were big Sox sponsors," Gaborek said. "Everybody else was Cub fans in 1969. I was a contrarian rooting for the White Sox."

Chicoine's father Walter was an engineer and salesperson, his mother Virginia was a homemaker. She grew up a Cubs fan on the South Side. "Mom knew all the players in the 1920s and '30s," Chicone said. "She'd go there on 'Ladies Day.' My Dad grew up on the North Side, but was a Sox fan."

Many of Chicoine's favorite vending anecdotes are from Comiskey Park. "Here's a great Disco Demolition vending story," he said. "When we came out of the commissary there were six vendors standing a couple of feet from each other. We were pouring as fast as we could to keep people away. We had one guy who we called 'Halpy' who was pulling stuff all the time. Very mischievous. He would give people bad change by misdirecting them, 'Oh, is that your friend over there?' He developed a moonwalk where he could be walking out of the commissary with a case of beer, appearing to be walking in so he didn't have to pay for it. Once at Wrigley, between games of a double-header all these guys are coming out of the john with full beers. We thought, 'What's the story here?' Halpy was actually in the john going up and down the troughs selling beer.

Vendor Bob Chicoine used Old Comiskey as a setting for a couple documentaries he produced, as well as his poetry, which has been published in several journals. He wrote about disco-era vendors like Mo: "Mo, the old man who took up his trade in the Depression because it seemed so romantic when the blue air all day, and two bucks commission would make your night at the honky-tonk." "Jesus spent three years in the wilderness; well I spent forty years in the ballpark. And now that I'm ready to preach I've got no teeth, my only gospel is my memory, and anyway who in my right mind would listen to this?"

"At Disco Demolition one guy stuck his claw into Halpy's case of beer and got away with one. Halpy throws down his two cases and heads into the crowd after the guy. His customers are still standing there. They just dive on the cases of beer and twenty seconds later there's no beer left. And Halpy comes back thirty seconds later. He didn't find the guy. He goes, 'What happened?' We go, 'Halpy, we tried.' But we didn't try. He had it coming."

Chicoine doubts Disco Demolition would have exploded in New York or Los Angeles. "By the time that disco hit in Chicago—a couple years later than the coasts—it was more glomming onto a scene than discovering a scene," he explained. "So for most guys who bought into that scene, the whole [*Saturday Night Fever*] Tony Manero hair/thread/dance moves thing was really putting on an act to score. South Side kids were envious of the conquests these guys were having, but in general saw it as fake, dishonest, beneath them, or too difficult—especially the dancing-with-a-partner part—to pull off successfully.

Gaborek sighed as he looked around the patio of the Morrie O'Malley's. "I remember how unplayable the field was after that game," he said. "I think that put the first hammer on the nail of Bill Veeck selling the team [after the 1980 season]."

Bill Veeck Appreciation Night was held September 30, 1980, at Comiskey Park. The crowd of 18,903 gave Veeck a two-minute standing ovation. Poor health kept him confined to the press box where he quipped, "The ballpark is obviously better preserved than I am." This would be Veeck's final appearance at the old dance hall, before he started hanging out in the center field bleachers at Wrigley Field.

The Loop staff in the Bard's room before Disco Demolition

Darlene "DJ Lady D" Jackson

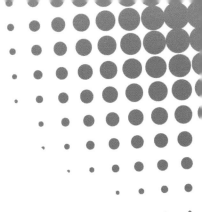

18. HOUSE

After the smoke cleared, Disco Demolition birthed Smart Bar and Metro, the historic alternative music rooms on the North Side of Chicago. The late Frankie Knuckles spun the narrow target of Disco Demolition into the freedom of house music.

With the same passion Steve Dahl brought to pulling the plug on disco music, Chicago music impresario Joe Shanahan has championed Chicago house music, arguably the most important musical export from the city since urban blues.

Shanahan is from south suburban Evergreen Park, about eight miles south of Old Comiskey Park. He opened Smart Bar in the summer of 1982 in the shadows of Wrigley Field. The dance club was on the fourth floor of the former Swedish Community Center, built in 1927. Frankie Knuckles was his first DJ. Shanahan then paired the intensity of house with the industrial music of Chicago bands like Ministry who played tapes of new material in the club.

Knuckles, who died in March 2014 at age fifty-nine, moved to Chicago from his native New York in the late 1970s. He told the *Chicago Tribune*, "I witnessed that caper that Steve Dahl pulled at Disco Demolition Night and it didn't mean a thing to me or my crowd. But it scared the record companies, so they stopped signing disco artists and making disco records. So we created our own thing in Chicago to fill the gap."

During a birthday party at Smart Bar in January 2015, Shananan said, "And there's no EDM [electronic dance music] without house. House is the genesis of something that went much bigger. Disco Demolition pushed the good disco culture further underground and that was a good thing. It gave birth to music that wasn't to be on *Dance Fever*. House has a rhythm that is body movement, and because it is bass heavy it moves the air. Great systems were being designed back then, and the original Smart Bar had one, the high end had such a sharp snare, the crack of a high hat was piercing. What existed in the middle was the mid tempo or some of the vocals, but it was really the high end and the low end that were so crisp, clean, and body moving."

Knuckles was given total freedom on his opening night at Smart Bar. Deploying two turntables and a reel-to-reel, he mixed The Police's 1980 instrumental-trance "Voices Inside My Head" with the rhythms of jet planes and tugboats along with samples from Dr. Martin Luther King's "I Have a Dream" speech as the vocal bed. It would not be a stretch to call Knuckles the minister, and his audience the congregation.

Knuckles' use of Dr. King's speeches influenced Tyree Cooper of DJ International Records (located in the shadow of the Cabrini Green Housing Project) who dropped in passages from the Reverend T.L. Barrett, Jr. of the Chicago Church of Universal Awareness, harvested from his mother's record collection.

"Frankie was the maestro," said Shanahan. "Frankie invented something unto himself. He would use a Talking Heads song or The Police alongside his personal remixes of classic disco of the time, like First Choice or Double Exposure. But he would strip it down so it wouldn't be like commercial radio. That's a wicked track, a minimal techno record. At that point, the Joe Shanahan-Frankie Knuckles relationship was solid gold. I was his promoter for thirty-two years. Smart Bar. Metro. I rented the Power Plant from him to do events for the Wax Trax! anniversary party."

Knuckles had left the Warehouse in 1982 to open his own club, the Power Plant, which closed in 1987. "Frankie was a great businessman," Shanahan said. "He was a global ambassador of our civic culture."

House was a stripped down disco.

Nile Rodgers explained, "House was another way of describing dance music, and a new decade's responsibility to come up with something new and clever. Obviously early house and disco are so married. House is disco's younger brother. Same thing with hip hop—disco's younger brother."

Bernard Edwards' bass riffs from "Good Times" were sampled in the 1979 single "Rapper's Delight" by the Sugarhill Gang. Members of the Sugarhill Gang heard Chic play "Good Times" in the fall of 1978 when the band appeared with The Clash and Blondie at the Palladium in New York City.

Rodgers reflected, "Unknowingly the Sugar Hill Gang was paving the way for the future. Now records are more like 'Rapper's Delight' than they are like 'Good Times.' More records today use samples as part of their grooves, they certainly use interpellations, and that's because they can shake up the electronic media and remove it or replace it with something that gives it a similar vibe. In the old days, we had to hear something, remember it and then try and incorporate it into our song. All musicians are inspired by other musician's compositions. We take them and rework them.

"David Bowie used to say, 'I don't call it stealing. I call it a post modernistic reinterpretation of an original idea.' I go, 'Yeah, Bowie, we're lifting the beginning of the Isley Brothers, 'Twist and Shout' for the beginning of 'Let's Dance,' note for note, bro."

Shanahan said you could feel the inhale and the exhale within the early days of Chicago house. "It wasn't disco to the point of Tavares', four on the floor, high-hat driven thing," he said. "It was more of a puff-puff. It was body music. It wasn't radio music. I do remember the Hot Mix 5 on WGCI and WBMX, and they would do house mixes. You would hear cars driving by with the windows down. We all loved Ralphie Rosario [of the Hot Mix 5] who did these house style disco records. He was at [the gay dance clubs] Broadway Limited and Paradise and he had this sound. Like Frankie, he was a DJ who was an artist and you'd go, 'That's where I want to be!' I think about the first house records, like Frankie's 'Your Love' with Jamie Principle [on vocals]. That's a wicked track, a minimal techno record." After Knuckles' death in March 2014 "Your Love" climbed up to number twenty-nine on the U.K. singles chart, topping the number fifty-nine position of the original 1989 U.K. release.

Darlene Jackson, DJ Lady D, grew up along 99th Street in the middle class neighborhood of Washington Heights on the far South Side of Chicago. Her mother Reola was a nurse and her father Ira was a machinist for thirty-five years at Stewart-Warner. Jackson's five brothers and sisters were born in the 1950s. She is the post-disco baby of the family, born in 1969. "By the time my parents got to me, they were fully invested in the middle class," she said. "I had it good."

Her brothers were DJs at community block parties and house parties. They kept a top notch hi-fi set in the basement of their home. "They'd say, 'Don't bother our stuff,'" she recalled. "As soon as they left, of course I was all over it. My brothers were into rock and funk. Two of my sisters were big into disco. Diana Ross was huge. I wanted to be a disco diva. I'd put on my mom's wigs and dance around the house in high heels. And negligees. I was just a kid during the height of disco. I used to cry because I couldn't go out with my sisters. I used to watch them getting ready, putting on their fabulous disco clothes. They used to go to the Copperbox and the 369 Club. I really liked Chic. My other sister was into singer-songwriter stuff. So I heard everything. I remember playing the turntables, music and records from the age of three. It was so amazing to me.

"My brother's rock influence was just as amazing to me as anything else. He had a Yes album. My sister played piano and she had Led Zeppelin sheet music so I was tinkering around with that stuff, playing finger notes."

Joseph Haley, the founder of the Jackie Robinson West Little League team, was vice principal of her elementary school. "It was a great community," she said. "Families knew each other. Most of the families were two parent households. It was an idyllic upbringing. We rode our bikes in the streets, we jumped rope. We were just east of Beverly, so we would venture over there and we'd get to see the upper middle class. It gives you a little more to aspire to. We weren't that far from Roseland either, so you would see what you didn't want.

"We went on a lot of vacations. I probably saw about forty-two states by the time I went to high school. We got in the car and drove. Big Cadillacs. On the road, from here to California. Route 66. My parents were into blues and jazz and country and western and that's what was rolling through the eight-track player on these vacations. We'd get to Nebraska and you'd get things like [Glen Campbell's cover of the Allen Toussaint song] 'Southern Nights' come across the radio."

Jackson never aspired to a career in music.

But while attending Whitney Young, the Hot Mix 5 would play at sanctioned parties in the school gymnasium. The Hot Mix 5 were the popular Chicago-based DJ conglomerate of Farley "Jackmaster" Funk, Mickey "Mixin'" Oliver, Scott "Smokin'" Silz, Ralph Rosario, and Kenny "Jammin'" Jason. They were hosts on the popular *Saturday Night Live Ain't No Jive* mix show on now-defunct WBMX-FM.

"At that time house had just exploded," she said. "It was 1982, my freshman year. A lot of people I knew had turntables at this point. Mixing had taken off, and being a DJ wasn't seen as a hobby, but as something people really did. I didn't think much of it, even though I started buying my own [records]."

Jackson went to Millikin Univesity in downstate Decatur, Illinois, where she graduated in 1990 with a BS in Biology, putting music on the back burner. After college, Jackson returned to Chicago where she worked jobs in retail, as an administrative assistant, and as an aerobics instructor. "I started going to parties at the club Shelter and the Boom Boom Room [at the Red Dog in Wicker Park]," she said. "That's when I fell in love with the art of being the conductor and making people do these things—almost like a puppet master. I was dating a DJ and we moved in together [at Atrium Village, Division and Wells on the near North Side]. Turntables came with the package. Eventually, the more time he spent away from the house the more time I spent with the turntables. In a couple of years I was out there doing it as well."

In 1995, Jackson moved in with three other DJs in a 3,000-square feet loft space at 120 North Green, which was a neighborhood known for its house music lofts. House DJs Derrick Carter and Mark Farina were also living in the building on Green during the early 1990s. The club Alcatraz and the second version of the

DJ LADY D PICKS FIVE ESSENTIAL HOUSE TRACKS DELIVERED FROM DISCO

1. Machine -"There But for the Grace of God Go I"
Tthis 1979 disco track was redefined as house in the house underground. Not every disco track had reach into house playlists like this one. I'm sure it's been played more in the house scene than it ever was in disco clubs. People still play it to this day. In 1996, Love Tribe had a huge global house and dance hit that sampled it, "Stand Up."

2. Farley Jackmaster Funk featuring Daryl Pandy - "Love Can't Turn Around"
From 1986, based on Isaac Hayes' "I Can't Turn Around," an early up-tempo soul tune [from 1973] that birthed not one, but two house tracks that competed with each other for status with house music fans. Farley Jackmaster Funk's "Love Can't Turn Around" featuring Daryl Pandy is an interpretation that sampled Hayes, and J.M. Silk's version is an outright housed-up cover version of Hayes' tune. With Pandy's vibrant and unforgettable vocals, Farley's more original interpretation became a house classic.

3. Any Italo disco song ever
The Italians were making hot, quirky, European sounding disco in the late 1970s and early '80s that segued itself into the house music landscape rather easily. Tunes such as "Dirty Talk" by Klein + MBO, "I'm Hungry" by S.T.O.P.P., "Hypnotic Tango" by My Mine, and "Feel The Drive" by Doctor's Cat defined the pumped up synth and drum machine new disco sound heard in Chicago's early house parties (1982, '83, '84).

4. Any Hi-NRG Song ever
Taking cues from the Italo disco movement, Hi-NRG came out of America, based on the Moroder disco sound. Hi-NRG inspired artists such as Bobby "O" Orlando to craft tunes such as, "She Has A Way" and "I'm So Hot For You," and to produce Divine's "Native Love" and the all-girl group, The Flirts, that spawned "Calling All Boys," among other underground house hits around 1983. This take on disco is also very much attributed to the Sylvester and Patrick Cowley Hi-NRG/disco sound "Mighty Real" (late 1970s) that was very popular in gay nightlife as well.

5. Chip E. and K. Joy - "Like This" (1985)
Sampling ESG's "Moody," this post-disco song made by an all-woman band from the Bronx in 1981, whose members were three musical sisters. Both tunes were played heavily in the house scene.

Warehouse were in the neighborhood. At the time, Jackson guessed there were no more than one female house DJs across the country.

"When we were younger, underground was probably paramount," she explained. "House was something you didn't want the masses to know too much about. Between 1990 and '96, we didn't have any type of presence in the media, and that was okay. There was a huge following. When you would see people who found their way in, they would have to be vetted and go through a period where they would be accepted into the fold. Nevertheless, you were a little bit excited when mainstream media got a hold of something. There were those moments in a year-end list where they might list the top clubs or top DJs in the city."

Jackson educated people on house by writing for the *Chicago Tribune*. She was one of the original Metro-Mix writers. "Things like club etiquette," she said. "If you came in and didn't know what you were doing you might offend people. Say a guy who went to hip-hop clubs came in. He goes into a house club and there's all this freedom. People are dancing all over the place and getting crazy—there's a feeling of not being judged. People who were new to that, it was a little bit shocking. Then they might take it too far and get too handsy or too grabby. That's not what it is. This is freedom of expression, but you still have to respect my personal space. You don't come in knowing these things."

The freedom of house music and its disco roots is an evolving, fluid topic for Shanahan. "It lives on!" he exclaimed. "You would go to clubs where those guys were spinning and you'd hear music not on the radio, not part of the mainstream disco world that I didn't like either. But I wasn't going to burn records. That was no way to prove my manhood. I'm proud of Chicago. When I saw a cultural move not sideways but backwards [like Disco Demolition], I was upset. Many of our friends were. We wondered why people were acting so weird towards us. Disco Demolition was a minority of hatemongers and using disco to be belligerent, drunk idiots."

Shanahan met Frankie Knuckles by hanging out at the original Warehouse. In 1979, Shanahan was gigging as a bartender at La Roulet, at 50 East Oak Street. He would work until three in the morning and head to the Warehouse with a couple of gay waiters and a couple of women to blow off steam. Shanahan would be train spotting to see what records Knuckles was playing.

Knuckles saw Shanahan often and eventually invited him into the DJ booth. Back on the day shift, Shanahan's boss at La Roulet was the late Chuck Fegert, *Chicago Sun-Times* vice president of advertising and marketing who was married to Barbara "I Dream of Jeannie" Eden.

"Actually, I went to Chuck and Barbara and said, 'Your weekday business is way off,'" Shanahan recalled with a bewitching smile. "Let me promote the Monday night. I guarantee you X amount of dollars at the bar and I'll take the door. I turned it into this hybrid of dance and punk rock. We called our company The Emotion Sisters and my roommate John Sulack and I did consecutive Mondays for several months. We brought in a punk DJ from Wax Trax! and a disco DJ. It was a hybrid of black, white, gay, straight, drag queens, and motorcycle guys. That was the boiler plate for Smart Bar. When I began to draw 500 people a night to East Oak Street, [I realized] this great culture existed in Chicago. I opened Smart Bar in 1982 on the premise that there was a hybrid of punk and dance."

Shanahan was thrilled that Knuckles would open the room. He recalled, "By this time he's my friend. When he told me his guarantee I was like, 'What?' He said, 'Well, how much do you pay a band?' I said, 'You got a point there.' I knew he was an artist. I paid him what his fee was. At the time I had no reference to that, because no one made more than a couple hundred bucks in the loft and party DJ scene I was involved in. We also had an event downstairs (in what was then called STAGES) which was the first Chicago appearance of [electro funkateers] Afrika Bambaatta with Soulsonic Force. I knew then I was on the right path. He said, 'Joe, I'm not sure the North Side is ready for this.' I said, 'Frankie, the Warehouse is at Clinton and Jefferson.' He thought it was far away. He didn't know if his crowd would follow him. I said, 'Your crowd that comes to see you regularly is my crowd. They will be there for us. You're going to see some new faces.' And that's what happened. We had a capacity crowd night that night. It was legendary."

According to Shahanan, "house" got its name by landing at the Imports Etc. record store in the South Loop. Customers had to enter the store through a garage. "Imports Etcetera was the important 'South Side' store—we called it South Side because it was south of Madison [in Printer's Row]," Shanahan said. "We'd go in and say, 'What was that track Frankie played at the Warehouse?' There was a bin and it said, 'Warehouse.' It became shortened to 'House.' That's the first time I recognized it was a 'thing.' I knew the music was unique; they were rhythm tracks of trains and jet planes. It was really druggy. You'd be in there and hear this supersonic jet go through the room and this incredible sound system and a tribal rhythm track behind it. This is where I wanted to be. I didn't want to be at Mother's listening to 'Play That Funky Music White Boy.'"

Darlene Jackson recalled a time when the house scene was a bit more heavenly. "When I go to clubs today, usually just to play, I find that kids today really lack club etiquette," she said. "A scene like Shelter was very free and party all night. What you were going to wear was going to be so different from the next person, where today that is frowned upon. You all need to look like Kim Kardashian with your straight hair, a blow out, a tight, tight dress and high heels. We didn't really have a uniform. It was all about how differently you can express yourself. It is very liberating once you discover it for yourself, and if you choose that it can open up a lot of possibilities for you.

"When it came to house music, the most important thing was to be open minded."

Comiskey Park in the aftermath of Disco Demolition

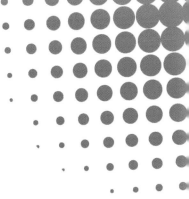

19. AFTERMATH

Steve Dahl was a willing and honest participant in this book because he wanted to set the record straight. He believed the racist and homophobic tones of Disco Demolition were amplified after he did not participate in a 1996 VH1 documentary *The Seventies*, a look back at the decade's popular culture.

"When I was at WMVP [in Chicago] I quit because they cut my salary in half," he explained. "I was supposed to do a VH1 interview because they did that series on the seventies. I forgot about it. The woman that produced it got super pissed. That documentary says Disco Demolition was racist and homophobic, I assume because I didn't show up—which I forgot about because I just lost my job. Blowing off that interview was a mistake. That's where it started. It was a cheap shot, made without exploration or documentation, and [it] served as a pivot point for their documentary. The VH1 special was the first time anyone reframed it in the [homophobic] light. And it became so."

Rock critic Dave Marsh was born in 1950 in Detroit, and was a cornerstone editor of the rock magazine *Creem*. In Tony Sciafani's thirtieth anniversary piece on Disco Demolition (to which Dahl did not respond to an interview request) Marsh said of the event, "It was your most paranoid fantasy about where the ethnic cleansing of the rock radio could ultimately lead."

Long time Chicago club DJ Joe Bryl reflected, "The gay scene was underground at the time. Boystown [near Wrigley Field in Chicago] is not what we're used to now. I don't know if it was a homophobic reaction, because gay culture was hidden from the mainstream. Most guys didn't know if their best friend was gay or not at the time. I just think it was a reaction to what they didn't like musically. In retrospect I think it was homophobic and racist. At the time I didn't. I've grown as a person to be more inclusive."

South Sider and Dusty Groove record store owner Rick Wojick said, "I didn't see Disco Demolition as racist, but you could feel there was an energy brewing—'We're taking something back.' Disco had become so mainstream by that point. It was on the charts." Bryl pointed out, "The top thirty or forty songs of that year were 75 percent disco-soul related. The only one that did better was the Knack's 'My Sharona,' which was more of a power-pop song. One of the positive things that came out of Disco Demolition is that it gave a push to the beginning of Chicago house."

Disco Demolition vendor Dave Gaborek sighed as he looked around the patio of the Morrie O'Malley's hot dog stand near U.S. Cellular Field. "I remember how unplayable the field was after that game," he said. "I think that put the first hammer on the nail of Bill Veeck selling the team (after the 1980 season)."

Over the years, Dahl also tries to find the positives and embrace the event:

In 1999 Dahl copyrighted the term "Disco Demolition." His attorneys filed a cease and desist order when Mike Veeck planned a twentieth anniversary Disco Demolition Night for the Tampa Bay Rays. In a 2004 interview with Thom Whatley, then Tampa Bay director of corporate sales told me, "We thought the letter was a joke. But it wasn't. They wanted to negotiate a rights fee to use the term 'Disco Demolition.' We said, 'Forget it.' We were just trying to have some fun."

Veeck said, "Today there's no relationship with Steve Dahl. I can't explain it. There's no hard feelings. He trademarked 'Disco Demolition.' The kids in Tampa Bay wanted to have fun with it. I said, 'Sure, let's do it.' And I got a cease and desist letter. Yeah, I had a lot to do with it too, but I didn't trademark it."

For the twenty-fifth anniversary of Disco Demolition, an eight page promotional "Disco Demolition" book was released and featured reprints of the original evening's pre-game program notes. The book was sponsored by Bud Light, Super Cuts, Chicago & Northwest Indiana Chevy Dealers, and others. The back of the book declares "Disco Still Sucks!" (July 12, 2004). At the time, Dahl was on radio station WCKG (105.9) FM.

Also in 2004, Dahl released the hour-long TV movie/documentary "Disco Demolition: The Real Story." The Baseball Hall of Fame and Museum in Cooperstown asked for the war helmet Dahl wore during the event. "It is going to be in a display about contemporary baseball culture," Dahl said. "It was in my basement hall of fame." Dahl grinned and said, "It is currently on loan."

Former WLUP promotions director Dave Logan said, "It is an event everybody knows. I was interviewing for a job at a radio station. I was sitting with all the corporate people at the table. They go, 'Tell us about your most successful radio promotion.' It's like playing softball and seeing it come at you in slow motion. Disco Demolition was sizematic in its impact."

Former WLUP publicist John Iltis remarked, "It was a good thing for The Loop. In those days we had a newspaper clipping service. I filled three books. It took us a month just to put the books together. One book was just from foreign press. As bad as it was, it was great PR. Steve's career really took off." The recognition didn't hurt Iltis either. His next big account was the opening of the Planet Hollywood restaurants.

John Iltis

Former WLUP general sales manager Jeff Schwartz said, "It is still a top 100 baseball moment. It would never happen today. Too many lawyers would say, 'Don't do it.' But we weren't smart enough to think that through. It took on a life of it's own. We were like the old philosophy, 'I'd rather be lucky than good, and if you can be both, you're going to win ninety-nine out of one hundred times. There is no embarrassment needed or shared for Disco Demolition."

Chicago artist and author Tony Fitzpatrick reflected, "There's a very good movie like *Dazed and Confused* to be made about Disco Demolition. I feel bad it was so difficult for Mike Veeck after that. But I believe in their hearts neither Mike Veeck or Steve Dahl had any intention of impeding anybody's sexuality or race. I haven't spoken to Steve in at least ten years, but it wasn't on Steve's mind. For him, it was a question of whether rock 'n' roll radio was going to exist. For me, Disco Demolition was a license to let your freak flag fly. We took over a ballpark. It was kind of cool. We began to realize we had a tiny bit of power in the world."

Dahl reflected, "I presented my kids' births on the air, had a live vasectomy, held a star-studded 'It's a Wonderful Life" and 'A Christmas Carol' (radio) plays and traveled all over with the first satellite remotes. Disco Demolition faded as a defining moment for me. It was a lap on my journey in radio."

But it is only fitting for Janet Dahl—his steadfast companion in life and music—to have the last word.

"Steve is a mysterious man," she said as she chose her words carefully. "He doesn't leave his deepest emotions out there. With his Dad dying in 2014, you plumb new depths and peel off a lot of layers. I think he is very guarded and suspicious of everyone. His Dad was kind of like that. Steve always has a plan. And he's more concerned about executing his plan than what anyone else thinks. He's glib, sometimes he writes people off and then I'm the person that can try to help him walk it back. You see, Steve thinks that saying nothing mean is the same as being supportive. But it's not.

"Everybody craves validation"

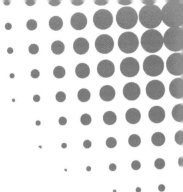

STEVE DAHL is an American radio personality, humorist, and podcaster. Born in California, he is the owner of the subscription-based Steve Dahl Podcast Network and broadcasts weekday afternoons on WLS-AM. A member of the Radio Hall of Fame, Dahl broadcast from Detroit stations WABX and WWWW before moving to Chicago in 1978, where he worked for WCKG, WDAI, WLUP, WMVP, and WLS. He served as a columnist for the *Chicago Tribune*, has appeared in several films, and is considered a pioneer in talk radio influencing many other radio personalities. Dahl resides in the suburbs of Chicago with his wife Janet.

DAVE HOEKSTRA is a Chicago author and producer. He was a columnist and critic at the *Chicago Sun-Times* from 1985 through 2014, where he won a 2013 Studs Terkel Community Media Award. He is a weekend radio host at WGN-720AM Chicago. Dave has written books about soul food and civil rights, Midwest supper clubs, and Minor League Baseball. He has contributed pieces to *Chicago* magazine, the *Chicago Reader*, and *Playboy*.

PAUL NATKIN learned photography in the trenches, working with his father, the team photographer of the Chicago Bulls in the late 1970s. He shot sports in the Chicago area for five years before he discovered music photography in 1976. He has toured the world with The Rolling Stones, Keith Richards, Brian Wilson, and many others. He also served as the official photographer of the Oprah Winfrey Show from 1986-1992. He has photographed magazine covers for *Newsweek*, *Ebony*, *Spin*, and *People*. See his work online at www.natkin.net.